1935 JUL 3 AM 8 39

SP X50 PHILADELPHIAPA 51 6.45PM 2ND

    LC MRS JAMES CROMWELL

        CARE MANUEL QUEZON YACHT SEABELLE

           DUE MANILA JULY FOURTH

DEAR DORIS DELIGHTED YOUR PROPOSED ADDITION MALMAISON DECIDED

MAURICE FATIO ONLY COMPETENT ARCHITECT HE CABLES BLOMFIELD AND

IS PREPARING PLANS YOUR APPROVAL WHERE SHALL WE MAIL THEM

THOUSAND THANKS DELICIOUS TEA HOPE YOU ARE RESTED AFFECTIONATELY

                    EVA STOTESBURY

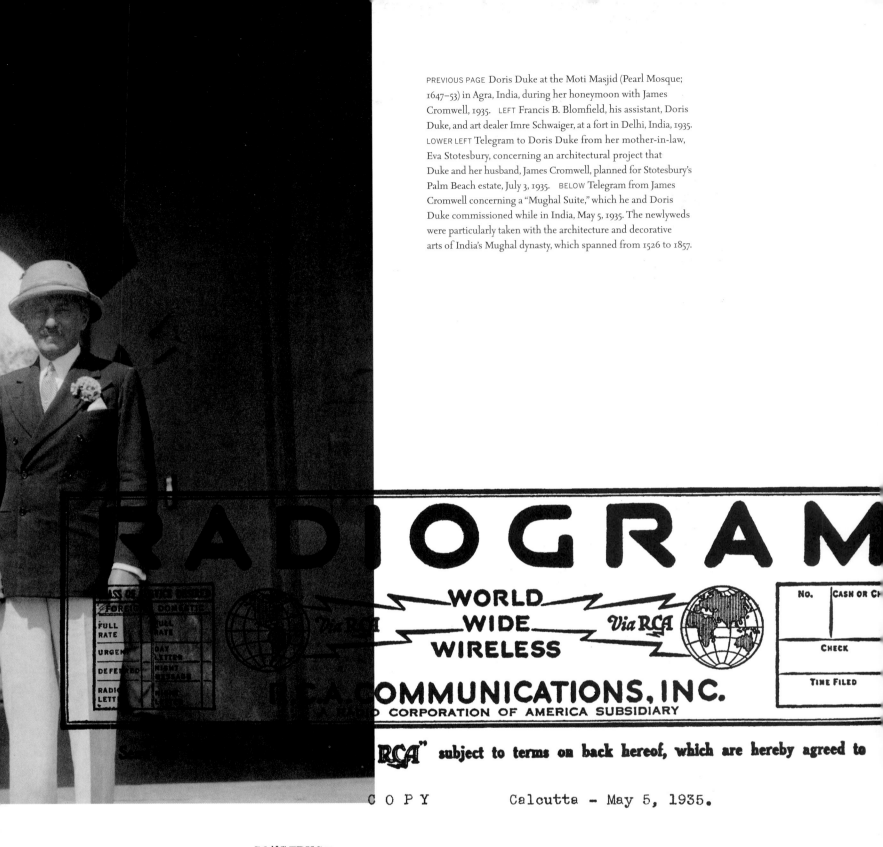

PREVIOUS PAGE Doris Duke at the Moti Masjid (Pearl Mosque; 1647–53) in Agra, India, during her honeymoon with James Cromwell, 1935. LEFT Francis B. Blomfield, his assistant, Doris Duke, and art dealer Imre Schwaiger, at a fort in Delhi, India, 1935. LOWER LEFT Telegram to Doris Duke from her mother-in-law, Eva Stotesbury, concerning an architectural project that Duke and her husband, James Cromwell, planned for Stotesbury's Palm Beach estate, July 3, 1935. BELOW Telegram from James Cromwell concerning a "Mughal Suite," which he and Doris Duke commissioned while in India, May 5, 1935. The newlyweds were particularly taken with the architecture and decorative arts of India's Mughal dynasty, which spanned from 1526 to 1857.

COPY   Calcutta – May 5, 1935.

CONSTRUCT,
Delhi.

This confirms request place orders immediately covering bathroom
complete and all Jali doors and windows STOP Mrs. Cromwell
thinks bedroom should have plain marble border but is worried
lest architraves over-doors and carved marble arch over beds too
ornate STOP We leave Singapore fifteenth – could you airmail
us rought sketches plain bed-arch, also Jali doors with and
without architraves, and your advice. Please wire Oriental
Hotel, Bangkok.

                    Cromwell.

Doris Duke and others embarking on a research and collecting trip to Iran, 1938.

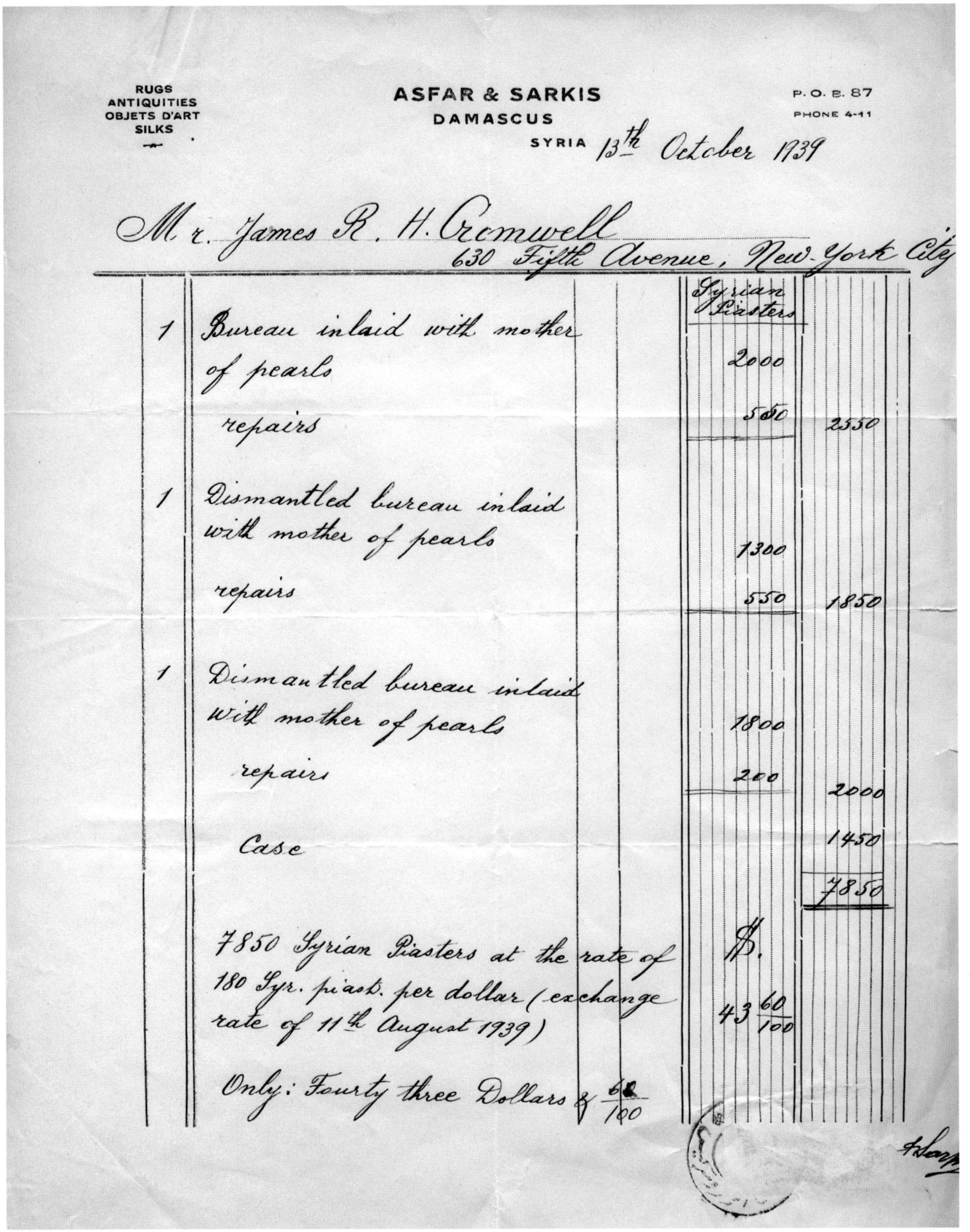

ASFAR & SARKIS
DAMASCUS
SYRIA

13th October 1939

Mr. James R. H. Cromwell
630 Fifth Avenue, New-York City

			Syrian Piasters	
1	Bureau inlaid with mother of pearls		2000	
	repairs		550	2550
1	Dismantled bureau inlaid with mother of pearls		1300	
	repairs		550	1850
1	Dismantled bureau inlaid with mother of pearls		1800	
	repairs		200	2000
	Case			1450
				7850

7850 Syrian Piasters at the rate of 180 Syr. piast. per dollar (exchange rate of 11th August 1939)

$. 43 60/100

Only: Fourty three Dollars & 60/100

TOP View of the bedroom wing under construction at Shangri La, 1937.   BOTTOM The entry courtyard at Shangri La, 1938.   RIGHT Doris Duke and Olympic swimmer Sam Kahanamoku at the entrance to Shangri La, 1938–39. Doris Duke met the Kahanamoku family on the final stop of her around-the-world honeymoon, and they became lifelong friends. The extended family, including Duke Kahanamoku, who is credited with popularizing surfing beyond Hawaiʻi, introduced her to the culture of the pre-statehood islands.

PREVIOUS SPREAD David Kahanamoku, Doris Duke, and James Cromwell (with Sam Kahanamoku in the foreground) fishing in the ocean below Shangri La, 1939.   ABOVE Sam Kahanamoku, Doris Duke, James Cromwell, and Chick Daniels in Waikīkī, 1935–37.   RIGHT Doris Duke and her crew await the start of a canoe race in Hawai'i. From left: Sam Kahanamoku, Doris Duke, Bill Kahanamoku, and Sargent Kahanamoku, 1936–37.

Doris Duke and James Cromwell pose by the Jali Pavilion at Shangri La, 1939.   FOLLOWING PAGE Doris Duke at Shangri La, 1939.

DORIS DUKE'S
SHANGRI LA
A HOUSE IN PARADISE

ARCHITECTURE
LANDSCAPE
AND
ISLAMIC ART

EDITED BY Thomas Mellins and Donald Albrecht

FOREWORD BY Deborah Pope

ESSAYS BY Linda Komaroff, Keelan Overton, Sharon Littlefield Tomlinson,
and Thomas Mellins and Donald Albrecht

ORGANIZED BY the Doris Duke Foundation for Islamic Art

PRINCIPAL PHOTOGRAPHY BY Tim Street-Porter

Skira Rizzoli
NEW YORK

CONTENTS

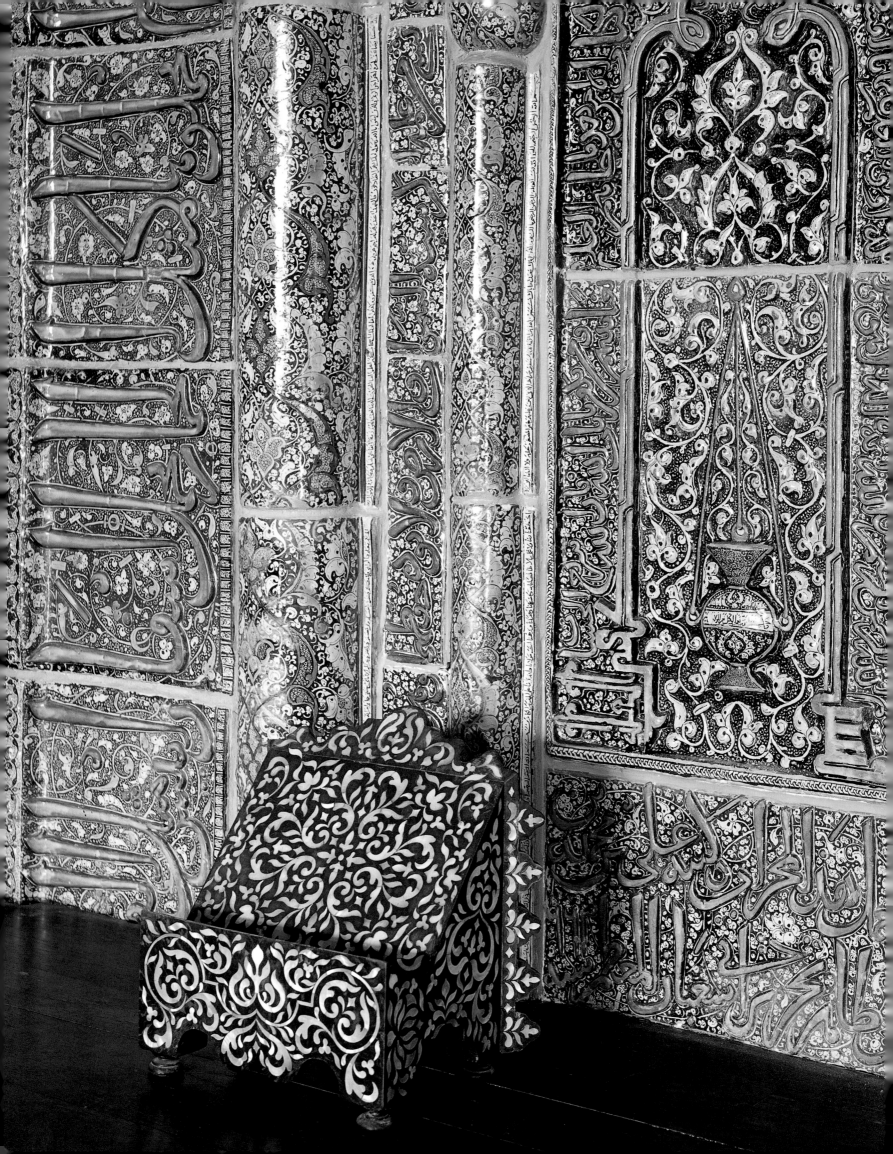

In 1947 Doris Duke wrote an article "My Honolulu Home" for *Town & Country*, which was accompanied by a glorious suite of black-and-white photographs by Maynard Parker. Published as one of only three photo shoots of Shangri La that Duke permitted during her lifetime, "My Honolulu Home" granted the curious public a glimpse of the most personal and secluded of retreats. Built between 1936 and 1938 and embellished with new acquisitions and renovations for nearly sixty years, Shangri La seamlessly melds 1930s modernist architecture; architectural traditions from India, Iran, Morocco, and Syria; and a large collection of Islamic art.

Duke recognized that Shangri La is a place of many identities: It is elegant, complex, embracing multiple traditions, and difficult to characterize. Calling it "a Spanish-Moorish-Persian-Indian complex," she shyly acknowledged Shangri La's fluid identity, paying homage to a Pan-Islamic world and representing the cultures, art, and architecture that it comprises. That she managed to build such a house and set it on southeastern Oʻahu's rocky coastline overlooking the Pacific, resolving such seemingly contradictory elements, is testament to her unerring eye and intuitive sense of the places and traditions she loved.[1]

Doris Duke left behind little in the way of personal correspondence and no diaries, but she otherwise kept extensive records that included invoices, household inventories, photographs and film, business correspondence with architects and art dealers, and architectural drawings and renderings. These written records and images together with Shangri La have shaped our understanding of Duke's work: the inspirational travels in the Islamic world, designing and building, and collecting and commissioning artwork. These stories are now told in a variety of voices and images throughout this book and the exhibition it accompanies.

In her will, Duke purposefully opened the doors to Shangri La by establishing the Doris Duke Foundation for Islamic Art (DDFIA) to own and manage the site and collections for the purpose of promoting the study and understanding of Islamic arts and cultures. The process of preparing this private, very intimate home for a broader public purpose is one she set in motion thirty years before her death. Renovating the dining room to a tented interior, installing a dazzling painted room from Damascus in the late 1970s, and continuing the expansion of the collection are all physical evidence of Doris Duke at work: deliberate, thoughtful, and joyfully unconstrained by narrow, essentialist thinking.

Today, Shangri La is alive with visitors and programs; artists and scholars in residence; performances of music, dance, and poetry; and international convenings and symposia that consider contemporary issues or advance research on aspects of Islamic art. The indoor and outdoor rooms of the site fill with conversation about the art and architecture, the views, and the work of the collector. With this traveling exhibition and book, *Doris Duke's Shangri La*, we take a similar experience to audiences beyond Hawaiʻi's shores and hope that the story of Shangri La and Duke's transformative engagement with the Islamic world will inspire a new appreciation of Islamic arts and cultures.

DEBORAH POPE
Executive Director, Shangri La, Doris Duke Foundation for Islamic Art

PAGE OPPOSITE TABLE OF CONTENTS
Detail of painted wood panel decorated with floral and fruit designs, Damascus, Syria, early eighteenth century.

LEFT Detail of mihrab (prayer niche) from the Imamzada Yahya at Veramin, Iran. Made in Kashan, Iran, dated Shaʻban AH 663/May 1265 AD, signed ʻAli ibn Muhammad ibn Abi Tahir. Stonepaste: molded, underglaze painted in blue and turquoise, overglaze painted in luster, 151 3/8 x 90 x 8 1/2 in. (384.5 x 228.6 x 21.6 cm). In the Mihrab Room.

A mihrab orients the faithful toward Mecca during prayer. At Shangri La, the mihrab marks the eastern terminus of the property's dominant east–west axis.

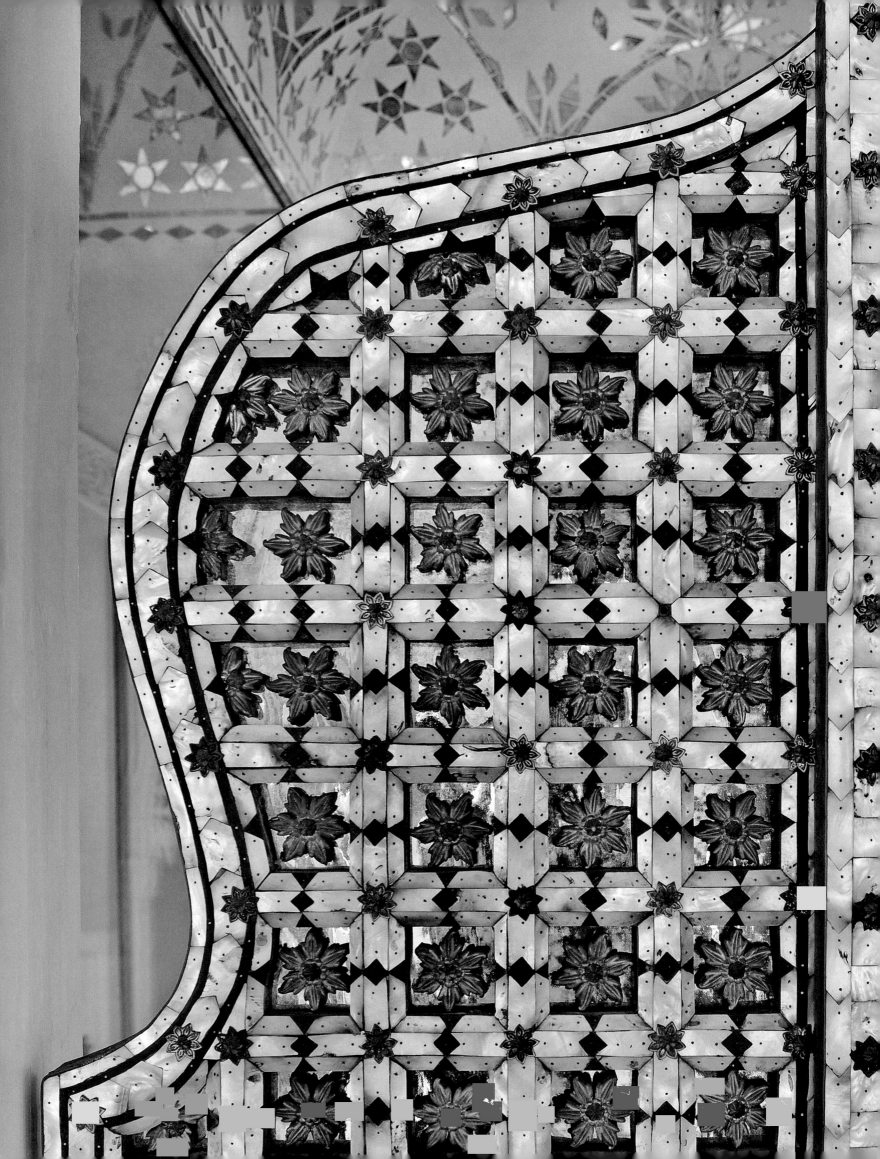

EDITORS' NOTE AND ACKNOWLEDGMENTS

This book and the exhibition it accompanies, *Doris Duke's Shangri La*, explore Duke's five-acre Honolulu estate through various avenues. The book begins with a suite of newly commissioned photographs by Tim Street-Porter, which visually convey Shangri La's seamless integration of architecture, landscape, and Islamic art. Following this visual introduction, three essays examine the evolution of Duke's collections. Linda Komaroff positions Duke within the context of an earlier generation of collectors, while Keelan Overton focuses on three seminal trips that Duke and her husband, James Cromwell, took to research and gather collections for Shangri La. Completing this trio of essays, Sharon Littlefield Tomlinson analyzes two complementary strategies by which Duke integrated her collections into the estate. After a portfolio of selected objects from Shangri La, our contribution, the final essay, focuses on Shangri La's architecture and design, placing it within the contexts of both modernism and the aesthetic preferences of Duke's social milieu.

In organizing the exhibition and editing this book, we have relied on the efforts of many individuals. The book's essayists have generously shared their knowledge and expertise, helping to lay the framework of the entire project. Tim Street-Porter's photographs offer the next best thing to visiting the house itself. We thank Abbott Miller and his colleagues at Pentagram, Susan Brzozowski, Brian Raby, and Kim Walker, for their lively and evocative design of both the exhibition and the book. Ileen Gallagher creatively and skillfully directed the exhibition's national tour. During a research trip to Palm Beach, we were aided by Scott Moses, Director of Library Services, Preservation Foundation of Palm Beach, and Debi Murray, Chief Curator, Historical Society of Palm Beach County. Fred Eckel gave us valuable background on Palm Beach architecture, also serving as a tour guide to its treasures. At Rizzoli, both publisher Charles Miers and editor Sandy Gilbert Freidus were instrumental in making this book a reality.

This project was fully supported by the Doris Duke Charitable Foundation and the Doris Duke Foundation for Islamic Art. We acknowledge the contributions of Maja Clark, Collections Manager, Shangri La; Kate Papazian, Program Associate for Strategy and Planning, Doris Duke Charitable Foundation; Mary Samouelian, Doris Duke Collection Archivist, David M. Rubenstein Rare Book and Manuscript Library, Duke University; Elizabeth Steinberg, Archivist, Doris Duke Charitable Foundation; and Dawn Sueoka, Consulting Archivist, Shangri La. We also thank the photographer David Franzen and editor Erin Barnett. We are especially indebted to Deborah Pope, Executive Director of Shangri La, who provided essential information and guidance throughout the entire project and served as a most gracious host to the property. Finally, we are grateful to Ed Henry, President and CEO of the Doris Duke Charitable Foundation, and Peter Simmons, the foundation's Chief Operating Officer, who, along with Deborah Pope conceived of the project and stewarded it through every phase of development and production, ultimately bringing it to fruition.

THOMAS MELLINS AND DONALD ALBRECHT

Detail of a nineteenth-century northern Indian door in the dressing room of the Mughal Suite.

SHANGRI LA

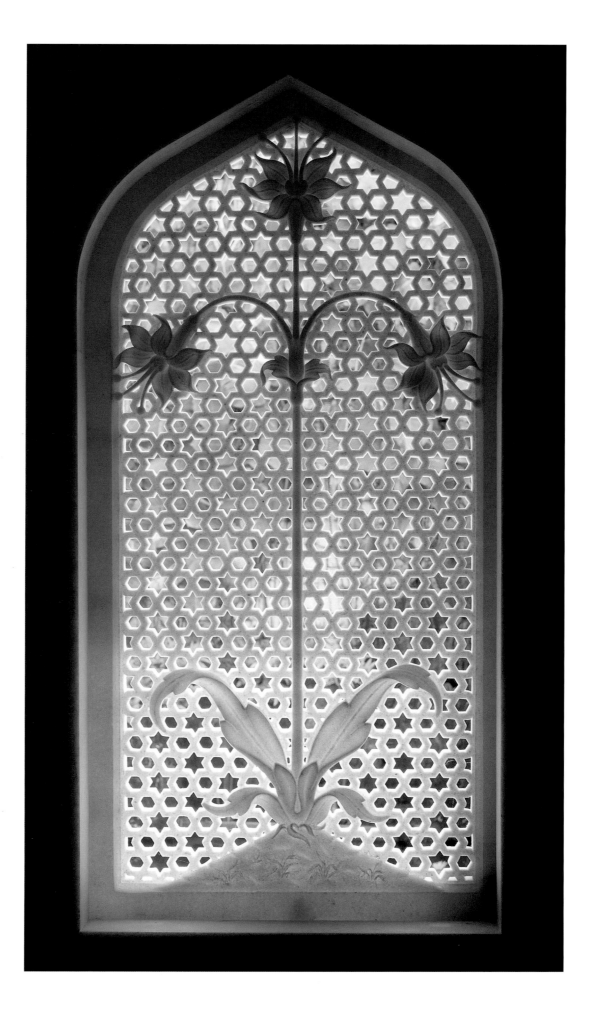

I met Doris Duke just once. It was in Malibu at an informal Sunday lunch on the ranch of decorator Tony Duquette. Doris was reserved but friendly—tall, slender, and sphinxlike. She had asked Duquette, an old friend, to do some decorating work in her Los Angeles residence, Falcon Lair, and once lunch was over, there they were in an adjoining room—two exotic elderly individuals mulling over fabric samples. This chance encounter reawakened my interest in Shangri La, which I knew little about except that Duquette described it as "quite extraordinary." Shangri La began to take on mythic dimensions in my imagination—all the more so because the sprinkling of existing photographs taken by Horst and others were nothing less than tantalizing. Collectively, however, they fell short of giving any real sense of what it was like as a place. It had never been fully documented, and I hoped that one day I would have that chance.

My opportunity came in 2010. Wendy Goodman, the New York design writer and editor, called to say that she had just been to Honolulu and visited Shangri La. It had been restored and she felt it would be an excellent time to call the very friendly director, Deborah Pope, and plan a visit. Wendy was wonderfully right, and better still, Donald Albrecht and Thomas Mellins had just visited the house to conduct research for the traveling exhibition that they were curating. After meeting with them and talking to my publisher Charles Miers at Rizzoli, it was decided to launch this book, featuring my newly commissioned photographs, to coincide with the exhibition's opening in New York.

It was soon arranged that I would stay in the Playhouse on the property. And so it was that in March of 2010 I flew to Honolulu and found myself, late in the evening, at the gates of Shangri La. I was to treasure every minute. The weather was perfect, and everyone at Shangri La most helpful. I spent happy hours in the vaults below the house, exploring the rows of racks filled with Duke's collections, which had been accumulated over nearly six decades of collecting, as well as the impressive subterranean machine, built by the Otis Elevator Company, that hydraulically lowers the enormous plate-glass windows separating the living room from the gardens.

At nighttime and over the weekend I had the property all to myself. All that was missing was Doris herself—but there were plenty of anecdotes about this most idiosyncratic person, who did not fit in with any conventional stereotype of a wealthy heiress. I loved it when I was taken on an initial tour, and I asked if she had used the lawns for croquet. "Oh no," was the reply. "This is where she played touch football with her Hawaiian surfer pals."

TIM STREET-PORTER

PAGES 8–9 Aerial view of Shangri La.

10–11 Entry courtyard.

12–13 Foyer.

14 Pierced metal lamp in front of the wood grill, custom-made in Morocco in 1937–38, that screens the central courtyard from the foyer.

15 The central courtyard looking toward the Mughal Suite.

16 A pierced metal lamp hanging from the Moroccan ceiling in the foyer.

17 Landing on the stairway connecting the central courtyard and the foyer.

18–19 Central courtyard.

20 Central courtyard column capital.

21 Central courtyard columns.
These cedar columns were fabricated in Chicago by the firm of Hartmann-Sanders, and the mirrors were applied in early 1941 by carpenter K. Fujii of Honolulu. The faceted capitals, column shafts faced with patterned mirrors, and sculpted bases are based on seventeenth-century prototypes in Isfahan, Iran, which the Cromwells photographed and filmed on their 1938 trip.

22 Syrian Room.
The acquisition and installation of the Syrian Room dates to the late 1970s–early 1980s. The space combines original eighteenth- and nineteenth-century architectural elements from Damascus (including calligraphic panels dated AH 1271/1854–55 AD), with new components created on-site at Shangri La. Many of the historic elements were previously installed in the Hagop Kevorkian Center for Near Eastern Studies at New York University.

23 The masab (decorative niche) in the Syrian Room.
Holding cherished objects, a masab was often a prominent feature in interiors from Damascus.

24 Mirrored doors in the Syrian Room.

25 Syrian Room.

26 Detail of Syrian Room vitrine with a sixteenth-century dish from Iznik, Turkey, two examples of nineteenth-century glass from Iran, and a seventeenth-century voided velvet panel from Turkey.

27 Syrian Room.

28 Marble fireplace in the bedroom of the Mughal Suite.

29 Vitrine in the living room.

30 Table, Kashmir, probably nineteenth century. Carved and painted wood, 25 1/4 x 17 3/8 in. (64.1 x 44.1 cm).

31 Powder room adjacent to the living room.

32 View into the living room from the central courtyard.

33 Living room.

34 Detail of mace, Iran, nineteenth century. Steel, 30 1/8 x 3 1/8 x 2 3/4 in. (76.5 x 7.9 x 7 cm). In the dining room.

35 A marble fireplace from Spain, probably thirteenth century, is flanked by fifteenth–sixteenth-century Spanish luster chargers and a frieze of luster tiles, all acquired from sales of the William Randolph Hearst collection in 1941. A coat of arms, a gift to James Buchanan Duke from the Turkish ambassador, hangs over the mantle in the living room.

36 Living room, showing the glass wall leading to the garden.
Throughout Shangri La, Duke incorporated modern elements. The living room for example, features ceiling coves with indirect lighting and curtains and upholstery by Dorothy Liebes, a leading mid-century textile designer. The room also has a floor-to-ceiling glass wall (with screens closed); its individual panels retract into the basement.

37 An elaborately tiled arch framing the living room as seen from the Mihrab Room.

38 Shelves at the east end of the living room displaying Persian ceramic vessels and storage jars dating from the eighth to seventeenth centuries.

39 Moroccan doors in the living room leading to the Mihrab Room.

40 Dining room.

41 Dining room.

42 Dining room lanai atop the seawall.

43 Mosaic tile panel in the form of a gateway, Iran, probably nineteenth century. Stonepaste: monochrome-glazed, assembled as mosaic, 153 x 160 in. (388.6 x 406.4 cm). On the dining room lanai.

44 Private hall leading to the entrance of the Mughal Suite.

45 Private hall connecting the main house to the Mughal Suite.

46 Floor lamp, Egypt or Syria, late nineteenth century. Cast and pierced copper alloy (brass), 68 x 21 1/2 in. (172.7 x 54.6 cm). In the Mihrab Room.

47 Jali at entrance to the Mughal Suite.

48 Bathroom in the Mughal Suite.

49 Detail of the dressing room ceiling in the Mughal Suite.

50 Dressing room in the Mughal Suite.

51 Detail of the Mughal Suite dressing room.

52 Jali in the bathroom of the Mughal Suite.

53 Waterfall in the private garden adjacent to the Mughal Suite.

54–55 Mughal Garden.

56 Cascade in the Mughal Garden, with gateway leading to the entry courtyard.

57 Entry courtyard, with gateway leading to the Mughal Garden.

58 Mughal Suite.

59 Mughal Suite, showing the stairway leading to the Jali Pavilion.

60–61 Balcony off the Damascus Room.

62–63 Seawall with the Playhouse beyond.

64 Playhouse lanai.

65 Pool with the Playhouse beyond.

66 Detail of the stenciled ceiling and column at the Playhouse lanai.

67 Living room in the Playhouse.

68–69 Pool with the cascade and the house, looking east.

DORIS DUKE
AND THE ISLAMIC ART COLLECTING TRADITION

Linda Komaroff

This essay will consider Doris Duke as a collector of Islamic art within the broader context of other American collectors and collections. While individual taste, vision, and resources varied, Duke may be viewed as one among many prominent figures with an appetite for Islamic art. Like a number of these collectors—such as Charles Lang Freer, Edward C. Moore, H. O. Havemeyer, Henry Walters, and Arthur M. Sackler—she ultimately sought to share her passion with the public, as visualized through the unique creation of Shangri La. As with other such collections that have entered the public domain, the Doris Duke collection has in many ways been transformed from a private and idiosyncratic predilection to a body of material with the ability to influence scholarship and to help shape universal notions of Islamic art.

The history of Doris Duke's collection is closely intertwined with her own history. While nothing in her upbringing or education prepared her to assemble a collection of Islamic art or to create a distinctive space for its display, the circumstances and social milieu into which she was born carried with them the means and the impetus to collect. Indeed, art collecting in America, as elsewhere,

and in all of its permutations and specializations, is very much a complex and peculiar "social habit," one often restricted to those of great wealth or taste or both.[1]

The only child of the tobacco and electrical energy magnate and benefactor of Duke University, James Buchanan Duke, and his wife Nanaline Holt Inman, Doris Duke was born in 1912 at their French neoclassical–style mansion at Fifth Avenue and 78th Street, toward the northern end of what was then known as New York's "Millionaires' Row." The family also had homes at Duke Farms, in Hillsborough Township, New Jersey; Lynnewood Hall in North Carolina; and in Newport, Rhode Island, at the Rough Point estate, once owned by the Vanderbilts. James Duke died in 1925, bequeathing his daughter the bulk of his considerable fortune as well as the family residences. At twelve years of age, Doris Duke became known as the "world's richest girl."[2]

Duke was presented to society as a debutante in 1930, aged eighteen, at a ball at Rough Point;[3] at twenty-one she received the first of several large bequests from her father's will,[4] and at twenty-two she married James Cromwell, an aspiring politician and a member of the Stotesbury family of Philadelphia.[5] For their honeymoon in 1935, the couple embarked upon a ten-month world tour that included Egypt, India, Indonesia, China, and Japan; their trip ended in Honolulu. While the honeymoon trip and its final destination are the usual starting point for any discussion of Doris Duke's fascination with Islamic art and architecture, and it is certainly from this time as a married woman of great fortune that she had the freedom to explore fully her interests, she may have received inspiration earlier.[6]

In New York and elsewhere in America, collections of Islamic art were being formed from the later nineteenth century onward.[7] America's social elites, stimulated by Islamic-inspired installations at world's fairs and expositions, Orientalist paintings, popular travel accounts, and by their own travels, were beginning to discover Islamic art, although they may not have known it by that name. "Moorish," "Hispano-Moresque," "Saracenic," "Persian," "Turkish," and "Oriental" were terms more commonly and often indiscriminately applied. No American collector was restrictive in his or her methodology but acquired broadly and deeply, frequently without regard to geographical boundaries and cultural distinctions. For many of them, however, collecting was more than merely evidence of their command of wealth and social status; art collecting was seen to reflect discriminating taste and personal inclinations. Among the most prominent collectors to precede Doris Duke were Edward C. Moore, Charles Lang Freer, Henry Walters, and H. O. Havemeyer.

Edward C. Moore (1827–91) was a silversmith and chief designer at Tiffany & Co. from 1868 until his death.[8] He collected widely and largely for inspiration in his work as a designer. His personal collection of some four thousand objects, which were displayed in mahogany cases in a special gallery adjacent to his Madison Avenue mansion, comprised East Asian pottery, lacquer, metalwork, arms and armor, and jades; Roman glass; Greek vases;[9] and Islamic objects in a wide variety of media and many of which were acquired from important European collections and private dealers. (There is no direct evidence that he ever traveled to the Middle East.)[10] Moore bequeathed around one thousand five hundred objects to the Metropolitan Museum of Art, including some rare and spectacular examples of Islamic art, most notably enameled and gilded glass, carved and

PAGE 72 Doris Duke shopping for mother-of-pearl bureaus in a courtyard in Damascus, Syria, in 1938.

ABOVE Doris Duke and James Buchanan Duke in Europe, 1923.

TOP Unidentified man, Doris Duke, and James Cromwell in India, 1935.

LEFT Doris Duke at Ashoka's pillar in the Qutb Mosque complex (1193–1316), Delhi, India, 1935.

ABOVE Doris Duke and James Cromwell in Hawai'i, 1935.

inlaid wood, and gold and silver inlaid metalwork from thirteenth- and fourteenth-century Egypt and Syria.[11] The terms of Moore's gift suggest that he viewed these works as a totality and one that would benefit future generations of designers.[12]

Charles Lang Freer (1854–1919), who made his fortune in the railway car industry in Detroit, retired from active business at the age of forty-five to concentrate on travel and collecting art.[13] Freer's life as a collector is documented in part through his exhaustive correspondence with friends and advisors. Early on, he had developed an interest in the works of James McNeill Whistler; his friendship with Whistler and his growing collection of the artist's works led to an enthusiasm for Asian art. Freer saw these two collecting areas as entirely complementary.[14] He made multiple trips to Japan and China, which helped to expand his knowledge and his collection. Freer also became interested in Islamic art and especially ceramics, in particular wares from the north-central Syrian site of Raqqa, known for its striking underglaze-painted turquoise-and-black pottery as well as its lusterware.[15] In 1908 he traveled to the Middle East, where he acquired works of art and honed his skills in the connoisseurship of ceramics, noting in a letter home that this "information alone is worth more to my personal collection than I had dared to dream."[16] He also purchased from dealers, perhaps most significantly Dikran Kelekian (1868–1951), who sold Freer his first Raqqa ware.[17] Kelekian was one of several influential Armenian dealers who assembled large and important collections of Islamic art that helped to shape the history of the field.[18]

Freer built a stately home in Detroit to which he successively added two exhibition galleries to display his growing collection, the bulk of which was stored elsewhere.[19] By the opening years of the twentieth century, Freer had determined

LEFT Doris Duke arriving at the Newark airport at the end of her honeymoon trip, January 13, 1936.

ABOVE Doris Duke shopping for mother-of-pearl bureaus in a courtyard in Damascus, Syria, in 1938. Georges Asfar, the dealer from whom Duke purchased three such bureaus in October 1939, exits the frame on the far left. Also visible are Charles and Rose Asfar.

to give his vast collection of about thirty thousand works to the United States as part of the Smithsonian Institution and to provide funds to erect an appropriate structure to house it on the National Mall in Washington, DC. He played an active role in choosing the design of the building—a simple two-storied Italianate structure with a central courtyard—and in planning the galleries, which expressed his aesthetic philosophy, one in which there was a natural sympathy between his Whistler collection and his East Asian and Islamic collections. The Freer Gallery of Art opened to the public in 1923.[20] Among the terms of his generous bequest, Freer's decision not to allow any works of art to ever leave the building suggests that he sought to preserve his personal collecting vision in perpetuity.[21]

Henry Walters (1848–1931) inherited a railroad business and an art collection from his father William. Already a modest collector in his own right, within several years of his father's death in 1894, the younger Walters dramatically increased the breadth and scale of his acquisitions, resulting in an encyclopedic collection of twenty-two thousand works of art. He bequeathed this collection to the city of Baltimore in 1931, housing it in a palazzo-style building first called the Walters Art Gallery and now known as the Walters Art Museum. Much more so than Freer, Walters' collecting interests were shaped and expanded by his relationship with

LEFT Ali Qapu (1590–1643), Isfahan, Iran, photographed during the Cromwells' trip to Iran in 1938.

ABOVE Tile panel, Spain, ca. 1525–50. Earthenware: underglaze painted with blue and overglaze painted with luster, each tile: 9 1/2 x 10 in. (24.1 x 25.4 cm). In the living room.

the dealer Dikran Kelekian.[22] Walters and Kelekian had met in 1893, at the World's Columbian Exposition in Chicago, which represented the dealer's first foray into the American art market. Although he purchased wide-ranging works from Kelekian, which reflected his own personal tastes, Walters was encouraged and cajoled by the dealer to expand his interests to include Islamic art. To judge by the broad array and exceptional quality of the Islamic objects purchased from Kelekian, the collaboration between collector and dealer was highly successful. Kelekian's persuasive personality notwithstanding, Walters may have developed a genuine attraction to Islamic art, as he seems to have appreciated small-scale and exquisitely crafted objects. Collecting Islamic art also may have appealed to Walters as a reminder of his travels in the Middle East and as a way of making tangible the objects and imagery captured in the Orientalist paintings collected by his father and familiar to him from childhood. Whatever the reasons, Walters left behind a comprehensive collection of some one thousand two hundred examples of Islamic art.

The H. O. Havemeyer donation to the Metropolitan Museum of Art of nearly two thousand works of art, made at the time of Louisine Havemeyer's death in 1929, is famous for its roster of Old Master and Impressionist paintings.[23] Less well known is that the gift also included a large and diverse collection of decorative arts ranging from small-scale ancient Egyptian sculpture to Japanese folding screens and Islamic ceramics.[24] Henry Osborne Havemeyer (1847–1907), known as the Sugar King, was the dominant figure in the sugar refining industry in late nineteenth-century America; he began collecting even before his marriage to Louisine Elder (1855–1927) in 1883. Like many other Americans, H. O. Havemeyer first became acquainted with Asian art through the 1876 Centennial Exhibition in Philadelphia.[25] Louisine Havemeyer, on the other hand, became interested in Asian art as a teenager after visiting Whistler's London studio, not unlike Charles Freer.[26] A good deal of the Havemeyers' early collecting as a couple focused on the interiors of the neo-Romanesque mansion they built at 66th Street and Fifth Avenue, which was completed in 1892.[27] Their dining room walls were decorated with Spanish lusterware—so-called Hispano-Moresque pottery—and the ceiling of the library was composed of variously patterned Japanese silks overlaid with an Islamic star design of ebony, of which Louisine said it "recalled the art of the East in both color and design."[28] But perhaps the most remarkable aspect of the home's interior were the glass mosaic frieze panels circumscribing the main entrance hall, which repeated an Islamic-inspired design with arabesque, vegetal, and geometric elements, created by Louis Comfort Tiffany.[29]

The Havemeyers, adventurous and often astute collectors, were therefore already receptive to Islamic art even before their meeting with Dikran Kelekian at the 1893 World's Columbian Exposition. Their introduction was likely instigated by Louisine Havemeyer's closest friend, artist Mary Cassatt, with whom the Armenian dealer also enjoyed a long-term friendship. The Havemeyers seem to have developed an amiable relationship with Kelekian, which lasted the rest of their lives. When they traveled to Egypt in 1906, they were accompanied by Kelekian, from whom that same year they acquired a large group of Islamic ceramics and metalwork.[30] The dealer had access to archaeological finds from commercial

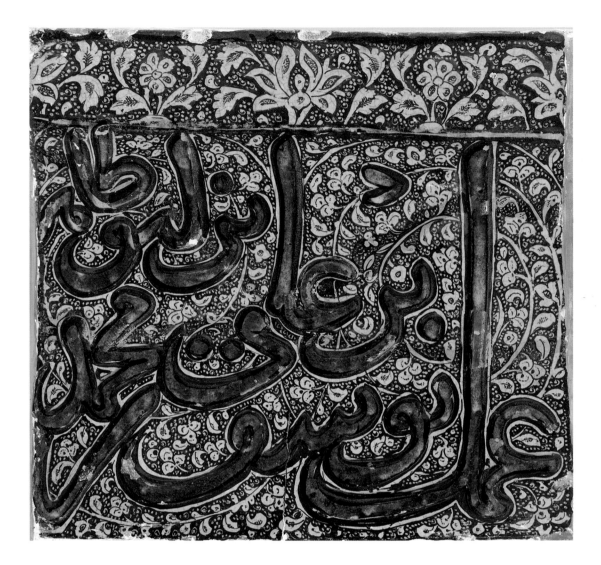

■ 192   GREEN GLAZED SAFAVID MOLDED BOTTLE, Isfa-
han, 1st half of the 17th century, of squat rectangular form with
stepped shoulders and funnel-shaped mouth, the sides with molded
panels depicting a maiden playing a tambourine and a kneeling youth
gazing at a dancing girl, *one crack - height 9 inches (23.8 cm.)*

Provenance: Enrico Caruso
            Phoebe Apperson Hearst

For reference to similar molded Safavid bottles with a green glaze see: A.
Lane, *Late Islamic Pottery*, London 1957, pl. 96 and 97; and C.K. Wilkin-
son, *Iranian Ceramics*, New York 1963, pl. 91.

■ 193   SAFAVID MONOCHROME BOTTLE, Kirman, 2nd
half of the 17th century, of ovoid form, with raised foot and short
neck, the olive green glaze with white floral sprays on either side, *foot
restored, neck cropped - height 8½ inches (21.6 cm.)*

■ 194   NINE QAJAR MOLDED TILES, Persia, circa 1900, each
square tile painted in polychrome, with molded decoration including
warriors in combat and architectural details - *each tile 8¼ inches (20.7 x
20 cm.)*

■ 195   ONE ABBASID STORAGE JAR, Syria, 8th/9th century,
the turquoise glazed vessel with ovoid body, sloping shoulder and four
strap handles, *considerable iridescence - height 15¼ inches (38.3 cm.)*

■ 196   TURQUOISE GLAZED BOWL, Raqqa, early 13th century, with bulbous body, slightly raised foot, straight neck and two
handles, painted with black designs over turquoise, *considerable iridescence - diameter 8 inches (20.3 cm.)*; Seljuk turquoise glazed bowl,
probably Sultanabad, late 12th/early 13th century, the interior
and exterior decorated with black scrolling foliate designs, the outer
border with band of molded calligraphy - *diameter 7½ inches (19 cm.)*
(2)

■ 197   ONE BROWN LUSTER JUG, Raqqa, 12th/13th century, with raised foot, pear-shaped body and pinched lip, the body
painted in radiating panels of brown luster divided by blue strokes,
restoration at top - height 7½ inches (19 cm.)

■ 198   AN UNUSUAL BLUE AND BLACK GLAZED BE-
AKER, Syria, 13th century, with flaring sides, the exterior painted
with three bands of black zig-zag decoration, *fragmentary - height 5½
inches (14 cm.)*

192

FAR LEFT One of a pair of panels decorated
with floral and fruit designs, Syria, Damascus,
originally part of the Metropolitan Museum
of Art's "Damascus Room," dated AH 1119/1707
AD. Painted and gilded wood, 110 1/4 x 25 1/4 in.
(280 x 64.1 cm). In the Syrian Room.

ABOVE Signature tile, from a set of ten tiles. Iran,
Kashan, probably 1310, signed Yusuf ibn 'Ali ibn
Muhammad ibn Abi Tahir. Stonepaste: molded,
underglaze painted in blue, overglaze painted
in luster, 15 5/8 x 16 1/4 in. (39.7 x 41.3 cm). In the
Mihrab Room.

LEFT "Fine Oriental Miniatures, Manuscripts,
and Islamic Works of Art," page from Sotheby's
auction catalog, dated December 10, 1981, and
annotated by Doris Duke. For this seventeenth-
century Persian bottle, see page 162.

FAR LEFT Panel, Central Asia or Iran, fifteenth century. Wood, 68 x 44 in. (172.7 x 111.8 cm). In the Syrian Room.

LEFT Detail of column capital, one of a set of six columns, Spain, fourteenth century. Marble, 86 1/2 x 13 1/4 x 13 1/4 in. (219.7 x 33.7 x 33.7 cm). In the private hall.

BELOW One of a pair of shaped carpets, Northern India, Kashmir or Lahore, mid-seventeenth century. Wool and cotton, 15 ft. 4 in. x 9 ft. 5 in. (467.4 x 287 cm).

excavations at several sites in Iran and at Raqqa in Syria, which made it possible for him to offer the Havemeyers exceptional and rare ceramics. Louisine Havemeyer continued to acquire from Kelekian after her husband's death; there is evidence to suggest that she came to share some of the dealer's intense passion for Islamic pottery and that she viewed Charles Freer as a competitor in collecting in this area.[31] She also seems to have encouraged her son Horace in this avocation; on at least two occasions she gave him Syrian pottery as gifts. These objects, along with others acquired by Horace Havemeyer, were likewise bequeathed to the Metropolitan Museum of Art.[32]

The collecting activities described above, which ultimately benefited several public institutions and introduced museum visitors to Islamic art, helped to shape the discipline of Islamic art in America through exhibition and study.[33] This seemingly unfettered acquisition of Islamic art was also part and parcel of the massive art-buying spree associated with the Gilded Age.[34] Though Doris Duke belonged to a new generation, she grew up, quite literally, in the long shadow of this artistic legacy. Just twelve blocks south of her childhood home, the Havemeyers' fortresslike mansion, with its exotic interiors, remained intact until it was torn down in 1930.[35] A short walk to the north was the Metropolitan Museum of Art, where the Edward C. Moore bequest first went on view in 1907 and where there were rooms dedicated to Islamic art from around 1910 onward.[36]

As would have befitted someone of her background, Doris Duke traveled abroad as a young child and as a teenager.[37] In May 1930 she was presented at Buckingham Palace along with several other American debutantes;[38] she undoubtedly had access to many of the great houses, which still preserved the Islamic-inspired interiors that were popular in England in the later nineteenth and early twentieth centuries.[39] She was in London again the following year with her mother, and it is tempting to suggest that she saw the great Persian exhibition at Burlington House, which was on view during the opening months of 1931.[40] The groundbreaking exhibition remarkably brought together more than two thousand works ranging from prehistoric times through the Islamic period.[41] Most importantly, if Doris Duke had seen the installation, she would certainly not have failed to notice the thirty-foot, reduced-scale replica of the monumental entrance portal of the seventeenth-century Masjid-i Shah, or Shah Mosque, in Isfahan, rendered in painted cloth and stucco,[42] from which tile panels were later reproduced for Shangri La. Probably more spectacle than scholarship, the exhibition left an important impact on the study of Islamic art, especially through the multivolume *Survey of Persian Art*, published several years later.[43] Both the exhibition and associated publication were engineered by Arthur Upham Pope, who has been described, and not entirely facetiously, as "the P. T. Barnum of Islamic art."[44] Doris Duke would make Pope's acquaintance some years later in connection with arrangements for her extended trip to the Middle East in 1938, when she visited Isfahan and was smitten by the tile revetment of the city's mosques and palaces.[45]

In attempting to contextualize Doris Duke as a collector of Islamic art, it is important to bear in mind that just as Shangri La was only one of her several homes, representing a singular aspect of a multifaceted life, so too was Islamic

FAR LEFT Ghalian (water pipe), Iran, late nineteenth century, signed 'Abu'l Qasim ibn Mirza Muhammad. Enameled gold, silver, wood, 9 1/8 x 5 7/8 in. (23.2 x 14.9 cm).

LEFT One of a pair of doors, Iran, Tehran, dated AH 1228 and 1813 AD, signed Muhammad Ja'far Shirazi. Wood, ivory, bone, brass, 86 1/4 x 42 3/4 x 1 1/4 in. (219.1 x 108.6 x 3.2 cm). In the living room.

LEFT Mihrab (prayer niche) from the Imamzada Yahya at Veramin, Iran. Made in Kashan, Iran, dated Sha'ban AH 663/May 1265 AD, signed 'Ali ibn Muhammad ibn Abi Tahir. Stonepaste: molded, underglaze painted in blue and turquoise, overglaze painted in luster, 151 3/8 x 90 x 8 1/2 in. (384.5 x 228.6 x 21.6 cm). In the Mihrab Room.

ABOVE Tile panel, Syria, Damascus, late sixteenth century. Stonepaste: underglaze painted, 21 1/4 x 32 3/8 in. (54 x 82.2 cm). In the Syrian Room.

ABOVE Georges Asfar in the eighteenth-century Syrian interior that would be installed as the Damascus Room at Shangri La in 1955. This photograph is dated August 1, 1954, prior to the room's shipment to Hawai'i.

RIGHT South wall of the Damascus Room as installed at Shangri La, 1999.

FAR RIGHT North wall of the Damascus Room, 1999.

art only one of multiple collecting interests, not unlike the collectors discussed above. For example, she devoted considerable energy toward Rough Point, the Duke home in Newport, especially after her mother's death in 1962, not only in terms of furnishing it with Old Master paintings, Flemish tapestries, and Chinese porcelains, but also in restoring it, through which she became concerned with the preservation of the other great houses of Newport.[46] But regardless of the original provenance or cultural affiliations of the acquisition, or how it was to be displayed or incorporated in one of her homes, Duke seems to have demonstrated supreme confidence in her choices and decisions.

Doris Duke's fascination with the Islamic world is demonstrated primarily through her creation of Shangri La, and while the sum of its parts is unique, in assembling many of its component works of art, she often echoed the tastes and inclinations of the earlier generation of collectors discussed in this essay. Her acquisition of Persian luster pottery and tiles and the colorful ware known as mina'i; colored glass bottles from Qajar, Iran; Turkish pottery and tiles from Iznik; Spanish lusterware; monochrome turquoise-glazed wares from Syria; Syrian inlaid wood furniture; and late Ottoman period rooms from Syria were all in keeping with earlier patterns of collecting in which decorative force triumphed over historical and cultural contexts.[47] Similarly, her focus on combining a diverse array of authentic works with new commissions to produce an "Oriental" ambiance relied upon a previous tradition.[48]

It is not easy to obtain a deeper sense of Doris Duke's special relationship with Islamic art and her interests in collecting, which likely involved some combination of personal, aesthetic, emotional, and intellectual responses to this material. Unlike other collectors, such as Freer or Louisine Havemeyer,[49] Duke left neither extensive personal communications nor memoirs that might reveal the rationale behind some of her choices and her aspirations for the collection. Apart from the collection, which cannot properly be disassociated from Shangri La itself,[50] the single most cogent document that speaks to the strength and depth of Duke's commitment to Islamic art is her establishment of the Doris Duke Foundation for Islamic Art in her will dated April 5, 1993, for which the basic parameters were already established in 1965: through Shangri La and its resources to "promote the study and understanding of Middle Eastern art and culture."[51]

RIGHT Doris Duke, 1930s.

COMMISSIONING ON THE MOVE

THE CROMWELLS' TRAVELS AND PATRONAGE OF "LIVING TRADITIONS" IN INDIA, MOROCCO, AND IRAN

Keelan Overton

On November 1, 2011, the Metropolitan Museum of Art in New York inaugurated its New Galleries for the Art of the Arab Lands, Turkey, Iran, Central Asia, and Later South Asia. One of the highlights of the fifteen-gallery ensemble is the Moroccan Court, a medieval-style courtyard featuring, among other things, a central fountain, zellij tilework (a mosaic technique consisting of monochrome-glazed tiles cut into geometric shapes), stuccowork, a cedar ceiling, and green roof tiles.[1] Nearly all components of this space were created by Arabesque, a workshop in Fez specializing in traditional Moroccan craft.[2] This project, which aims "to show the living traditions of the Islamic world," provides a contemporary point of entry into the exploration of Doris Duke and her husband James Cromwell's patronage of living craftsmen from throughout the Islamic world during the mid-to-late 1930s.[3] The Cromwells' commissioning efforts were deeply informed by their adventurous thirst for travel (India in 1935, Morocco in 1937, and Iran in 1938) and subsequent desire to re-create aspects of Islamic architectural ambiance within their Honolulu home, Shangri La. The latter goal often necessitated the ordering of custom-made architectural features from contemporary workshops. Here lies a series of intriguing parallels between their patronage in the 1930s and current trends in museum installations of Islamic art: the appreciation of "living traditions" and the impetus to, at times, preference architectural context over the individual object. This essay explores the circumstances of the Cromwells' patronage, one that can be compared to the recent Metropolitan project, and may even have concrete links to it, but which ultimately remains distinct.

The importance of "living traditions" in the history of Shangri La—rather than simply the acquisition of "historic" works of art—is exemplified by the fact that the Cromwells' first major commission *preceded* both their introduction to Hawai'i in August 1935, and subsequent conception of Shangri La. In late February 1935, near the beginning of their around-the-world honeymoon tour, the couple arrived in India.[4] One of the honeymoon scrapbooks assembled by James Cromwell reveals that the majority of their two-month stay was spent in the north: in Rajasthan, Agra, Delhi, Srinagar (Kashmir), Darjeeling, and Calcutta.[5] While in Agra and Delhi, Duke became enamored of Mughal architecture, particularly that of the reign of Shah Jahan (r. 1628–58). A photograph of her standing in the Moti Masjid (Pearl Mosque) of the Agra Fort seems to capture her musing over the translation of Mughal aesthetics into her own private world. Indeed, she soon resolved to commission a marble bedroom-and-bathroom suite (19 x 49 feet), one largely inspired by the Taj Mahal, for the addition being planned for Malmaison, her husband's lakefront house on the grounds of El Mirasol, the Palm Beach estate of his mother, Eva Stotesbury.[6] The suite's hallmark feature was to be a set of marble *jalis* (perforated screens), each of which constituted one element of a tripartite system of sliding units also including a mesh screen and a glass door. The couple also desired a rooftop garden "partly covered by awnings, which could be reached by a covered outside staircase, like the one on the south side of Almirasol [sic]."[7] Mrs. Stotesbury's response was positive, and she soon enlisted Palm Beach–based Maurice Fatio as architect of the exterior. For the Mughal-style interior, the Cromwells had already selected Francis B. Blomfield, a British architect they had met in India. Blomfield and his partner/elder brother C. G. Blomfield were well-known for a variety of buildings in Edwin Lutyens' New Delhi.[8]

The commission progressed rapidly during the Cromwells' stay in India. Soon after being engaged as designer, Francis Blomfield contracted the India Marble Works firm of Agra, self-declared "specialists in inlaid marble works and models of Taj," to create the marble elements. The substantial order included eleven *jalis* set within architraves (seven with geometric patterns for the bedroom and four with superimposed flowers for the bathroom), three additional architraves without *jalis* (one framing the bed), flooring, border elements, dado panels with floral designs in the *pietra dura* technique, a fireplace, and a bathtub with an elaborate arched

A BIT OF INDIA FOR FLORIDA

THE JAMES H. CROMWELLS
The former Doris Duke, heiress to many of the Duke tobacco millions, and her husband, photographed against the background of the Taj Mahal while on their 'round-the-world honeymoon.

DUKE MILLIONS SAVE HINDU ART

Cromwells Revive Indian Marble-Carving for Decorations in Florida Home

DELHI, India, May 29 (AP)—American wealth, drawn from the tobacco fortune of the former Doris Duke and her husband, James H. Cromwell, has saved India's ancient art of marble-carving as exemplified in the beautiful Taj Mahal.

Copies of some of the carved windows, inlaid doors and panels of the famous temple at Agra have been completed and are on their way to the United States to adorn a bedroom and bath in the Cromwells' palatial home at Palm Beach, Fla.

Ordered on Honeymoon

They were ordered by the couple while visiting India on their honeymoon last year, thereby providing an impetus for the centuries-old industry which had almost died out in modern times.

Only a few descendants of the craftsmen who fashioned the Taj Mahal in Shah Jehan's time still carried on a precarious living by making small inlaid souvenirs for visitors to the temple.

The marble panels, as ordered by Mrs. Cromwell, form a dado about two and a half feet high, with each panel a floral picture.

Jewels Fitted In

Experts pronounce the workmanship a miracle of skill. Semi-precious stones—jade, cornelian, agate, malachite, lapis lazuli and mother-of-pearl—are fitted into the petals of the flowers and the curves of the stems. The natural veining of the stone has been utilized to stimulate the markings of flowers and leaves.

The stones were cut to the minutest fraction, for no cement or adhesive material of any kind could be used to hold them in position.

The result is a transparency and brilliancy unrivalled, say experts, since the dynasty which produced so many marvels of architecture in India.

For the Bathroom

The panels will be installed in a marble bedroom and marble bathroom in the Cromwell home, with eight of the huge carved masterpieces going into the bedroom.

Traditional geometrical patterns of the Taj Mahal doors have been preserved, but with a novel effect produced by super-imposing carved designs of lilies, iris and other flowers on the background. Each door occupied the time of six men for three months.

In addition, there is a screen with the Scales of Justice, copied in minutest detail from the famous screen in Delhi Fort.

Stirred by the Cromwells' patronage to a dying art, several maharajahs are considering following their example by engaging the newly discovered craftsmen for special inlay and carving work in their palaces.

backdrop.[9] The marble was to be of the highest quality ("all white marble is to be first class pure white Makrana marble;" "the yellow marble is to be the best quality Jaisalmer marble;" "the green marble to be the best quality green Baroda marble"), and the craftsmen were expected to follow designs provided by Blomfield ("the in-laid work is to be in semiprecious stones exactly in accordance with the Architect's drawings and instructions").[10] In terms of design, Blomfield would later write that the floral patterns of the bathroom's *pietra dura* panels would be inspired by "actual inlaid work either at Agra or Delhi," while the four floral carvings of the *jalis* had been "taken from the dado panels in the main entrance to the Taj."[11]

Like much of their honeymoon, the Cromwells' marble commission attracted significant press. While the couple was in Singapore the *New York Post* proclaimed:

> American wealth, drawn from the tobacco fortune of the former Doris Duke and her husband, James Cromwell, has saved India's ancient art of marble-carving as exemplified in the beautiful Taj Mahal. Copies of some of the carved windows, inlaid doors and panels of the famous temple [sic] at Agra have been completed and are on their way to the United States to adorn a bedroom and bath in the Cromwells' palatial home at Palm Beach, Fla.[12]

In 1935 the Cromwells were certainly not the first, and far from the last, Westerners to become infatuated with the Taj Mahal, which had long been marketed as India's premier tourist destination.[13] The extent to which the commission did indeed "save" India's marble craft industry remains to be determined.[14]

The suite project took a drastic turn upon the Cromwells' arrival in Hawai'i and their subsequent decision to build a home on the island. Luckily, the plans for Palm

PAGE 92 Moroccan craftsmen making the living room's carved and painted cedar ceiling, ca. 1937–38.

LEFT Page from James Cromwell's honeymoon scrapbook, 1935.

ABOVE Taj Mahal (1622–28), Agra, India.

Beach were readily transferable to Honolulu. The concept of a rooftop garden, for example, was preserved in what would become known as Shangri La's "Jali Pavilion." In August 1936, after learning that many of the jalis had arrived broken, the Shangri La team (led by H. Drewry Baker) reconstituted the damaged examples as a rooftop pavilion, which ultimately paralleled the original intentions for Malmaison.[15]

In May 1937, while construction of Shangri La was underway, the Cromwells embarked on another lengthy trip: a two-month tour predominantly of Europe, the sole exception being a week in the French protectorate of Morocco.[16] One of the Cromwells' main contacts there was Nigel d'Albini Black-Hawkins, a British army officer who had settled in North Africa and whose German wife, Mary Auras, had earlier been a leading muse of the British painter Sir John Lavery. During the 1930s the Black-Hawkinses had a residence in Marrakesh, and Auras appears to have been particularly fond of Moroccan art.[17] In addition to spending time with the Black-Hawkinses, the Cromwells were also accompanied by Ruth Selwyn, a Hollywood actress whose husband, Edgar Selwyn, had written the play *The Arab* and later starred in its first film adaptation in 1915.[18] The newlyweds had earlier encountered the Selwyns at a New Year's dinner during their honeymoon stay in Los Angeles, and Mrs. Selwyn would later also join them in Iran.[19]

While in Morocco, the Cromwells traveled to Marrakesh, Rabat, Fedala, and possibly Tangier. In Rabat they visited the Kasbah des Oudaia, a medieval fortress that overlooks the meeting point of the Bou Regreg River and the Atlantic Ocean and is renowned for its picturesque blue streets. The southern portion of the kasbah is home to a late seventeenth-century palace (now the Musée des Oudaia) of the quintessential Moroccan type (central courtyard with adjacent rectangular rooms, whose arched entrances are framed by soaring wood doors). Next to the palace are the Andalusian Gardens, which received considerable attention in film footage taken during the trip. In an ensuing segment from the film, Selwyn and Duke relax on a ledge within the nearby Café Maure, still a popular tourist destination. In Fedala, today the decidedly non-touristic commercial port city of Mohammedia, the group enjoyed a leisurely afternoon of lunching and swimming at what appears to have been a large villa.[20] The duration of the film footage shot at this site suggests that the Cromwells were entranced by its gardens, tiles, rooftop pavilions, and white facades, all of which must have resonated with their vision for Shangri La.

While Nigel Black-Hawkins oversaw the Cromwells' order of custom-made carpets from Hadj el-Mahdjoub Bouzian, a carpet dealer located in Marrakesh's Souk Semarine,[21] it was likely Mary Black-Hawkins who introduced them to René Martin, a French expatriate based in Rabat who was the "Administrateur Unique" of a firm called S.A.L.A.M. René Martin. The activities of this business included interior design, the sale of historic Moroccan craft, and the creation of new work for a range of projects, including hotels, the Great Mosque of Paris (1922–26), and the Exposition Internationale des Arts et Techniques dans la Vie Moderne (Paris, 1937).[22] Martin was also an amateur draughtsman, and in 1938, he published a small booklet entitled *Images de Rabat*, which included nearly thirty of his drawings.[23] In the accompanying text, he conveyed his love of the quiet and unimposing city, which he viewed as the antithesis to prevailing Orientalist fascinations with odalisques (female slaves) and bazaar curios, among other things.[24] Shortly after its publication, Martin sent an autographed copy of *Images de Rabat* to the Cromwells,

Jali at the entrance to the Mughal Suite at Shangri La.

ABOVE Jali Pavilion at Shangri La, 1941.

RIGHT Bathroom in the Mughal Suite
at Shangri La.

who would have been familiar with its drawings, especially those of the Kasbah
des Oudaia, a site they too had documented.

While it is unknown if the Cromwells encountered Martin in Morocco in May
1937, they certainly met him two months later, on July 20, in the French Riviera
resort of Antibes. It was here, at the end of the Cromwells' European tour, that all
parties signed a document prepared on S.A.L.A.M. René Martin letterhead titled
"Estimate for decorations and furnishings for the villa of Mr. James H. R. Cromwell
at Honolulu." This document listed custom-made architectural features in three
media — stucco, wood, and ceramic — for four spaces at Shangri La — living room,
foyer, central courtyard, and James Cromwell's bedroom. The commission for the
living room included a variety of wood elements: a painted and carved ceiling, tall
doors, a fireplace mantel with an arched dias, divans topped by bookcases, and
sliding blinds. The proposal also called for friezes and spandrels in stucco, as well
as zellij tilework (for behind the fireplace dias). The foyer estimate was equally

complex and included a ceiling, studded doors, handrails, balustrades, and a large screen — all in wood — as well as stucco spandrels and windows inset with colored glass (chemmassiat) for the upper portions of the room.[25] A wall fountain in zellij tilework was slated for the central courtyard, while doors, a bed with bookshelves, a "pair of presses" for the display of arms and armor, and sliding shutters were intended for James Cromwell's bedroom (also known as the "Moroccan Room"). Portions of the order, such as the ceilings and colored-glass windows, were later compared to prototypes reproduced in Jean Gallotti's two-volume Le Jardin et la Maison Arabes au Maroc, a publication owned by the Cromwells.[26]

Like the Blomfield firm, S.A.L.A.M. René Martin was expected to both ensure the successful completion of the order and to propose its ultimate installation and presentation at Shangri La. Not surprisingly, the lead designer in charge of the project, one P. Vary (not Martin himself), gravitated toward uniformly Moroccan aesthetics, as exemplified by his watercolors of the living room and foyer.[27] Today, the most quintessentially Moroccan arrangement in the home is the eastern terminus of the living room, where the arch framing the Veramin mihrab is embellished with a stucco spandrel and flanked by two tall doors, which in turn lead upward to a stucco epigraphic frieze and the wood ceiling. Perhaps the most practical feature of the Morocco commission was a diverse collection of geometric latticework (mashrabiyya), which is traditionally employed as window screens and balcony railings.[28] Between the Moroccan mashrabiyya and the Indian jali, Shangri La's individual rooms were assured privacy, spatial demarcation, mood, and perhaps most importantly, airflow and cooling.

S.A.L.A.M. René Martin was originally located at 21, souk el Ghzel in Rabat.[29] The Souk el Ghzel was formerly a bustling market at the end of the rue des Consuls, a main street in the medina (old city). Today, much of the souk serves as a parking lot, but one can still locate number 21, a large building whose whitewashed exterior includes blue highlights and whose front door is tucked into the corner of a small square.[30] Upon passing through a door comparable to those made for Shangri La's foyer and walking up a curved staircase, one enters a sunlit yet covered courtyard with zellij and stuccowork that may date to the late nineteenth century.[31] The adjacent sitting room, by contrast, features a wood fireplace-bookshelf arrangement that is a hallmark of the French protectorate period (1912–56).

This large courtyard home was not only the headquarters of S.A.L.A.M. René Martin, but also the home of its eponymous proprietor, Martin, and a second Frenchman who lived on the ground floor, possibly Vary.[32] The influence of this domestic setting on Vary's proposals for Shangri La appears to have been significant. Indeed, close comparisons can be made between the fireplace-bookshelf scheme originally proposed for the living room's north wall and the arrangement in 21, souk el Ghzel. The custom-made work for Shangri La was ultimately a combination of traditional Moroccan craft and protectorate-period creative license. This is perhaps best exemplified by the framing of the living room's fireplace with a wood epigraphic frieze, one emulating fourteenth-century examples. This treatment differed markedly from the originally proposed curved mantle with geometric pattern, thereby conveying the Shangri La team's continual modification and refinement of designs provided by the Rabat firm.[33]

RENÉ-MARTIN

La Pointe des Oudayâs.

ABOVE View of the coastline of the Kasbah des Oudaia, Rabat, Morocco (from René Martin, *Images de Rabat*, 1938).

LEFT Entrance to Aux Merveilles de Marrakech, 14, souk Semarine, Marrakesh. During their 1937 trip to Morocco, the Cromwells purchased both ready-made and custom-made carpets from this store, located in the medina's (old city's) souk district. Today, the family business is run by the son of the dealer who worked with the Cromwells.

View of the living room, looking east.
The painted cedar doors and the carved
stucco spandrel, both part of the
1937 Morocco commission, frame the
Veramin mihrab.

ABOVE *Mashrabiyya* in the courtyard of the Bou Inaniyya Madrasa (1350–55), Fez, Morocco. This type of *mashrabiyya* was selected for the "shutters" of James Cromwell's bedroom, also known as the Moroccan Room. (See page 108 for a photograph of the shutters.)

RIGHT View of 21, souk el Ghzel, Rabat, Morocco. This large courtyard house—distinguished by its light-blue highlights—was the location of S.A.L.A.M. René Martin, as well as the proprietor's residence.

FAR RIGHT Courtyard of the Attarine Madrasa (1323), Fez, Morocco. The quintessential elements of medieval Moroccan architectural decoration—*zellij* tilework, stucco, wood, marble—can be seen.

The simple credit line "Rabat, René Martin" does not adequately account for the myriad voices and hands responsible for Shangri La's Moroccan commissions. Perhaps most silenced to date have been the Moroccan craftsmen who actually made the work. Thanks to a series of compelling photographs provided to the Cromwells, likely by Martin, we can appreciate these artisans and their contributions. One image captures two craftsmen working on the living room's ceiling, while another depicts a stately *maalem* (master) standing behind portions of the foyer's balustrade and the Moroccan Room's ocean-side screen. In a third photograph, two artists carve distinct panels of stucco, only one of which was ultimately selected for the living room. Several of the craftsmen in these photographs have been identified as being from Fez.[34] It has been further suggested that the stucco specialists were members of the notable Telmsani family, descendants of whom, the Najis, own and lead the Arabesque workshop responsible for the Moroccan Court at the Metropolitan Museum of Art.[35] While these assertions remain to be clarified, it suffices to conclude that a diverse cast of French and Moroccan individuals, probably split between Rabat and Fez, contributed to the substantial 1937 commission for Shangri La.

By the close of 1937, the Cromwells began planning yet another major trip: a six-week tour of the Middle East, including Iran.[36] In advance of this journey,

ABOVE Moroccan *maalem* (master) standing
behind portions of the balustrade made for the
foyer and the screen made for the oceanfront
facade of Shangri La's Moroccan Room, ca. 1937–38.

OPPOSITE PAGE, UPPER LEFT Moroccan craftsmen
making the living room's carved and painted
ceiling, ca. 1937–38.

OPPOSITE PAGE, UPPER RIGHT Moroccan stucco
specialists preparing models for Shangri La's
living room, ca. 1937–38. The epigraphic panel
on the right was ultimately selected and is
today installed below the commissioned ceiling.

OPPOSITE PAGE, BELOW Custom-made furnishings for Shangri La's Moroccan Room, as seen
in Morocco before shipment.

TOP Masjid-i Shah (Shah Mosque; 1612–ca. 1630), Isfahan, Iran. This congregational mosque inspired the majority of the tilework commissioned for Shangri La in 1938.

BOTTOM Detail of mosaic panels on the entrance portal of the Shah Mosque, Isfahan, Iran. Individual panels located at the base of the portal's large *muqarnas* (three-dimensional stalactite formations) inspired the panel in Shangri La's dining room and the pair of panels on the facade of Shangri La's Playhouse.

RIGHT Tile panel custom-made for Shangri La by a workshop in Isfahan, Iran in 1938–39. Stonepaste: monochrome-glazed, assembled as mosaic, 240 x 132 in. (609.6 x 335.3 cm). On view in Shangri La's central courtyard. This large panel is a replica of one of the pair on the entrance portal of the Shah Mosque.

the couple seems to have put a "freeze" on Martin and Vary's influence. The predominance of Moroccan aesthetics in Shangri La's interior design may have given them pause, and it is probable that they desired to play a more involved role in the patronage process, rather than rely on publications and the fieldwork of others.

The Cromwells' confidence and involvement as patrons culminated in the Iranian tilework commission.[37] Whereas they spent only a week in North Africa, the couple traveled throughout Iran for nearly a month. Once again Ruth Selwyn joined the adventure, as did another female companion, Mary Crane, a graduate student in Persian art at New York University's Institute of Fine Arts. During this third trip, James Cromwell's penchant for documentation reached an apex, and he meticulously recorded, through both film and photography, all of the buildings and cities that would subsequently influence the built landscape of Shangri La. These inspirations included the major mosques and palaces of Safavid Isfahan, the Shrine of Imam Riza in Mashhad, and the pre-Islamic site of Persepolis, the capital of the Achaemenid empire (550–330 BC).

In advance of the Iran trip, the Cromwells resolved to research historic tile designs that could serve as prototypes for the creation of new tile revetment for Shangri La, where historic tilework alone could not mask the expansive and idiosyncratically shaped walls. Once in Iran, attention focused on Isfahan's Shah Mosque (Masjid-i Shah, 1612–ca. 1630), a large mosque located on the city's renowned *maidan* (square). The Shah Mosque had recently been restored and had subsequently garnered international acclaim, largely due to the concerted efforts of Arthur Upham Pope, an American dealer, collector, and scholar of Persian art. In addition to being the first Westerner to photograph the monument thoroughly, Pope also re-created it for exhibitions in Philadelphia and London (1926 and 1931, respectively).[38] Given that Pope had organized virtually all aspects of the Cromwells' Iran trip, which was modeled on the earlier tour of American collector and patron Ada Small Moore, it is not surprising that the couple gravitated toward the Shah Mosque.

Long before they arrived in Iran, the Cromwells were strongly influenced by Pope and his immediate circle. In Paris in February 1938, on their way to the Middle East, the couple met Ayoub Rabenou, an art dealer who divided his time between Paris and Tehran. Pope had advised Rabenou to prepare examples of both "antique" and "modern" tilework for the American patrons.[39] The delicate floral and arabesque patterns of Persian tilework must have presented a refreshing alternative to the rigid geometry of Moroccan *zellij*, which the Cromwells repeatedly rejected despite ongoing pleas by Martin, with whom they also met in Paris.

During their visit to Isfahan two months later, the Cromwells drafted a preliminary contract with Rabenou for custom-made tilework, not unlike the agreement they had established with Martin approximately a year earlier.[40] The majority of the tilework was inspired by designs on the Shah Mosque, particularly its exceptional entrance portal. While some of the commissions were relatively straightforward replicas (consider the large mosaic in the central courtyard), others (consider the large "stepped" example, which was intended for the central courtyard but is now on view in the dining room), were a creative amalgam of individual panels on the mosque's facade.

Rabenou's role in the tilework commission was far less influential than that of his counterparts in India and Morocco. He was not engaged as an interior

designer and therefore did not conceive of, nor propose, the general appearances of individual rooms. Whereas we can accurately position F. B. Blomfield and Vary/Martin as key designers in Shangri La's history, Rabenou's role was confined to the logistics of the commission, including its complex shipment. By the time of the Iran commission, the Shangri La team — the Cromwells, architect H. Drewry Baker, and Mary Crane — knew what they wanted and needed, and they enthusiastically took the lead.

One final group of individuals involved in the Iran commission deserves mention: the ceramists who made the substantial lot of underglaze and mosaic tilework for Shangri La's central courtyard and the facades of the living room portico and the Playhouse. Like Martin, Rabenou sent the Cromwells photographs of the craftsmen at work on the order. These photographs were taken in Isfahan in March 1939, and many of them retain a theatrical and staged air. The craftsmen have been forced to "modernize" their dress for the camera, while narguilehs (smoking pipes) and languid poses — most prominent in photographs not reproduced here — concurrently freeze them in the past in a typical Orientalist cliché. As with the Moroccan craftsmen, the biographical details of most of the Iranian artisans remain to be clarified. Rabenou's inscriptions on the versos of the photographs do, however, provide some critical information, including the name of one of the workshop's masters, Ustad Muhammad.[41]

While the Cromwells were in Iran in the spring of 1938, the shipment of replacement Indian jalis was received in Honolulu.[42] That fall, thirty-six cases containing the Morocco commissions arrived. On Christmas Day, the couple moved into the Mughal Suite, which they praised as "the loveliest room of the kind that we have ever seen."[43] They would ultimately have to wait nearly a year and a half before the arrival of the Iranian tile, which was installed in the summer and fall of 1940. The Cromwells' commissioning had spanned four years and taken them to several of the most important centers of Islamic art history. The effort was a team one, not just between husband and wife, but also between the young couple and innumerable craftsmen, architects, designers, advisors, and dealers. The legacy of these combined efforts is an institution where early-twentieth-century Islamic art in traditional modes can be explored in light of personal, colonialist, Orientalist, and preservationist narratives. Although the craftsmen who created Shangri La's commissions are no longer living, the celebration of "living traditions" of Islamic art persists in perpetuity at the site.

TOP Isfahani ceramists at work on the 1938 tile commission for Shangri La. The central courtyard's grills are visible face down; a plaster backing was subsequently applied to secure the individual pieces of mosaic. This photograph, sent to the Cromwells by Ayoub Rabenou, was one of a series taken in Isfahan, Iran, in March 1939.

BOTTOM Tile cutters in the workshop responsible for Shangri La's custom-made tilework, Isfahan, Iran, March 1939.

COLLECTING FOR DESIGN

ISLAMIC ART AT DORIS DUKE'S SHANGRI LA

Sharon Littlefield Tomlinson

From 1937 to 1941 Doris Duke collected vigorously, searching Europe, the United States, the Middle East, and North Africa for furniture, tile panels, textiles, and decorative arts with which to embellish the interiors and exteriors of Shangri La. During these years, Shangri La was built to accommodate Duke's rapidly expanding collection. As purchases were made, however, it became necessary to alter the architecture in accordance with Duke's ideas for displaying objects. Conversely, she sometimes chose to purchase particular objects based on the opportunities for display that Shangri La's existing architecture afforded. Thus, architectural design was influenced by the objects collected, and the objects to be collected were assessed for their potential place within both built and natural environments. These complementary approaches were driven by Duke's commitment to site-specific collecting—or, collecting that is designed to fit a complex context as it also reshapes it.

The earliest designs by the architectural firm Wyeth & King show flamboyant architecture, representations of Islamic-inspired art, and selections from Duke's budding collection of Asian art, which she acquired on her honeymoon. (In 1919

the Palm Beach–based architect Marion Sims Wyeth had formed a partnership with Frederic Rhinelander King, who ran the firm's New York office.) One rendering, for example, shows the main house from the ocean side, its facade replete with rows of doorways reminiscent of architecture in Isfahan, Iran. The effect is dynamic but demanding. In a watercolor proposal, a minaret-type structure above the master bedroom projects boldly into the sky. In the living room, a mural of Isfahan's central square is shown painted on the north wall under a geometric ceiling and adjacent to it are arabesque-inspired door spandrels.

Each of these designs pays homage simultaneously to Islamic architecture and modern architecture, and the result strains like an uncomfortable marriage. Duke must have felt similarly, for soon after these proposals and others were offered, the design shifted so that commissioned works of original art (rather than representations of art) were to be set off by a starker and simpler architectural aesthetic, one that was indebted mainly to modern architecture with occasional, subtle evocations of Islamic and Iranian styles. The simplicity of the architecture can be difficult to discern today, for the art collection grew substantially in the succeeding decades, as did the plantings of tropical trees and shrubs. Shangri La's architecture is their canvas and may be obscured by their exuberance. But the choice of modern

PAGE 114 Detail of living room rendering seen below.

LEFT An early proposal by Wyeth & King for the facade of Shangri La as seen from the ocean, ca. 1936.

BELOW A rendering of Shangri La's living room, ca. 1936, shows Islamic-inspired designs in the geometric ceiling and door spandrels, as well as a mural depicting the *maidan* (square) in Isfahan, Iran, on the far right.

The view into what would become known
as the Mughal Garden, 1938.

architecture with discreet references to Islamic architecture was essential to the success of Shangri La and made it possible for architecture, art, and landscape to work in sync rather than at cross-purposes.

Duke's first approach — having the art collection shape the site's developing architecture — can be seen in the area that would become known as the Mughal Garden, one of Shangri La's most striking examples of the synthesis of art, architecture, and landscape. This long, narrow garden was originally entered through a simple, bamboo gate surrounded by newly planted vines growing on metal screens.[1] Over time, as the vines grew, the entry would have become a "living wall" of tropical plantings that bespoke the Hawaiian locale.[2] But no sooner had it been constructed and planted than Duke was considering a replacement in the form of a massive, nineteenth-century tile gateway.[3] Negotiations with Ayoub Rabenou for the gateway's purchase unfolded over an approximately eight-month period in 1939. Duke steadfastly desired it as the new entry for the garden, but she did not wish to pay too much for it.[4]

The change from "living wall" to historic, ceramic gateway introduced a relationship between art and nature into the garden and also established a commanding new architectural structure on the estate. The original bamboo gate and its surrounding vines were removed, and in 1946 a massive, whitewashed wall was built, upon which the tile gateway would be installed.[5] The larger entry was proportionally consistent with the maturing Chinese banyans and bird-of-paradise plantings that ran the course of the garden in a way that would have eventually overwhelmed the modest bamboo gate. In addition, the experience of arriving at the estate must have been completely transformed by the new wall.[6] Whereas previously the garden, with its plantings and metal screens, might have seemed to expand outward from the entry courtyard, the wall uncompromisingly created two separate spaces. The gate through which the garden was now entered framed the landscape for the viewer, offered tantalizing glimpses of it, and also produced a sight line to define its length emphatically. Visitors today continue to encounter the wall as a formidable point of arrival into the entry courtyard and the Mughal Garden.

In the late 1950s or early 1960s, the tile gateway was removed from the garden and relocated to the dining room lanai. The effect of the huge whitewashed wall at the head of the garden must have pleased Duke because she retained it permanently after she had the tile gateway de-installed.[7] A pair of tile spandrels was then installed at the front and reverse of the wall and, as a result, minor architectural modifications were made to its facades.[8] With the spandrels in place, the reason for the wall's particular shape and size would have been lost were it not for the surviving photographs, which reveal how its design was tailored to an object in the collection no longer associated with it. Although the wall no longer houses the tile gateway, its overall effect — to screen, to frame, and to reveal the garden — remains a powerful, defining architectural feature of the estate.

The gateway was not the only tile panel to prompt architectural renovations. As Duke collected and installed more tile panels from 1938 to 1941, the buildings, and to a lesser extent the landscape, were subsequently altered. Tiles were added in the foyer, living room, and the Mihrab Room, prompting varying degrees of

ABOVE Mosaic tile gateway as originally installed at the entrance of the Mughal Garden, ca. 1946. Its scale would have been more proportional to the maturing landscape than the bamboo gate.

RIGHT Mosaic tile panel in the form of a gateway, Iran, probably nineteenth century. Stone-paste: monochrome-glazed, assembled as mosaic, 153 x 160 in. (388.6 x 406.4 cm). On the dining room lanai.

ABOVE The newly made wall emphatically separates the Mughal Garden from the entry courtyard, ca. 1946.

RIGHT The whitewashed wall that was built to hold the mosaic tile gateway remains in place and continues to shape visitors' experience of the entry courtyard and Mughal Garden.

alteration to each room.[9] Of course, not every purchase made for Shangri La was finely calibrated to the site. Duke made many purchases that, although they offered display value, do not seem to have been considered specifically for their fit within the built environment. Glass vessels, portable ceramics, and metalwork contribute effectively to the overall aesthetic but were not necessarily chosen for site-specific reasons.

Shangri La's central courtyard reveals Duke's second approach, whereby the existing architecture drove her decisions about what to collect. The courtyard's strong, symmetrical layout and axial path prescribed that any embellishments to its walls must likewise conform to axial symmetry—a design tenet that Duke adhered to over the decades as the courtyard became increasingly ornate. To understand the transformation of the courtyard, it is first necessary to trace the experience of its architecture. A visitor to the property would typically enter the main house through the foyer, proceed down the staircase, and stroll through the central courtyard, destined for the living room, the dining room, or the outdoors. Entering the courtyard from a northerly vantage point, the visitor's eyes would be drawn to its focal point—the center of the south wall—and from that focal point, progressively outward to the east and west walls to terminate at the center of the north wall underneath the staircase. Embellishments to the courtyard's walls, therefore, would need to take the focal point at the south wall into account and be mirrored outward, around the courtyard, until reconnecting at the focal point in the center of the north wall. To do otherwise would have created a disconcerting imbalance.

To embellish the courtyard in axial symmetry, Doris Duke commissioned two tile-mosaic panels from an Isfahani workshop administered by Ayoub Rabenou in 1938 to the exact specifications of Wyeth & King's plan.[10] These were to be the focal points of the south and north walls. Four tile door spandrels and four mosaic grills were also commissioned to mirror one another on the south wall, or the east and west walls. It was decided that the remaining surfaces, predominantly the east and west walls, but also some of the south wall, would be embellished by plantings. In its earliest incarnation, before the tiles were installed, the space showed the roots of this aesthetic. Simple white walls are accented with dark, decorative woodwork and highlights from the then-small collection: In one photograph from spring 1939, a mother-of-pearl trunk purchased in Syria is at the center of the south wall; in another photograph of a similar date, a *suzani* textile purchased in India has replaced it. Vegetation is the main decorative medium, with potted plants grouped around a lawn and more "living walls"—in this case, tree fern bark housing displays of orchids, anthuriums, and other tropical plantings that indicate the Hawaiian locale. Paired banana palms flank the art on the south wall to emphasize the courtyard's axial symmetry.

The commissioned tiles arrived at Shangri La in the summer of 1940, along with a large quantity of seventeenth–nineteenth-century tile panels also purchased in Iran from Rabenou in 1938. The massive commissioned tile panel for the south wall, the grills, and the spandrels were installed soon after, as were the historic tile panels. These panels, which are an iconic component of the courtyard today, were originally grouped in four pairs at the base of both sides of the stairwell.[11] Whether purchased intentionally or coincidentally, the eight panels are of identical or nearly identical design, coloring, and size, and they are perfectly suited for use in the courtyard, where mirrored embellishments were needed. Two wide panels were stacked one on top of the other at the bottom ends

Tile panel in the form of a spandrel, Iran, probably late nineteenth century. Stone-paste: underglaze painted, 54 7/8 x 19 in. (139.4 x 403.9 cm).

ABOVE A suzani (embroidery) temporarily hanging on the south wall of the central courtyard
while the large mosaic tile panel—specifically
ordered for this space—is being made in
Isfahan, Iran, 1938.

BELOW In the original design for the central
courtyard, fern bark was laid against the east, west,
and south walls, with tropical vegetation set
within it, 1938.

of the stairwell. Additionally, two pairs of narrow, vertically stacked panels were located on the stairway leading up to the landing.[12] Thus with this grouping of eight panels, the desired mirroring was accomplished at the outer edges of the northerly elevation.

For reasons not known, the commissioned tile, which had been intended as the focal point of the north wall, was instead situated in an outdoor position on the main lawn, where for fifteen years it engaged in a dialogue with the grounds before it was relocated to its final position in the dining room.[13] In late 1941 an intriguing group of thirteenth-century tiles arrived, and these were chosen to be the focal point of the north wall under the wood screen that shields the stairway.[14] The tiles had been purchased in 1938 while Duke was in Iran and were among a large quantity of historic tile panels she acquired during that trip, but they arrived at Shangri La more than a year later than the commissioned tiles sent by Rabenou.[15]

The nature of these thirteenth-century tiles allowed Duke to follow the axial symmetry of the courtyard and to proceed with the installation in two phases, assessing a partial installation within the existing aesthetic before filling the pre-scribed space completely. This group of tiles is of continuous geometric design, allowing patterns to emerge, which are limited only by the proportions of the designated wall or by the actual number of tiles at hand. Duke was fortunate to have been able to purchase almost exactly the number of tiles that she would need to fill the prescribed space. And further, of the tiles she did purchase, the glazed ones filled the central area of the north wall as framed by the courtyard columns and the unglazed ones filled the remaining areas at either end. It appears to be happenstance that enough glazed and unglazed tiles were available to fill the central portion of the wall and be perfectly set off by the columns. The installation of the glazed tiles was attempted first and Duke must have found the effect successful but underplayed. Hence, she decided to add the remaining group of unglazed tiles to either side of the glazed group. Border tiles are scattered along the edges to fill in gaps, but the overall pattern is symmetrical. Although an apparent coincidence, architecture and art are very much in sync.

In the early 1940s, landscape, art, and architecture must have been well-balanced in the central courtyard, even with the grass removed to make way for the fountain. Nature and art were juxtaposed within a rather rigid architectural setting, but side by side they worked together to create dimension, texture, color, and interest. Yet in time, art would become the stronger focus, and while the landscape con-tinued to be key, it would complement the space rather than dominate it as it had in 1939. This did not mean that art had free reign, however. The appearance of the courtyard was entrenched, and whatever changes Duke made from then on would continue to serve the architecture's axial symmetry and the dominating presence of Iranian tile panels.

Perhaps due to an inability to maintain the grounds during World War II, it appears that around 1946—when Duke returned to Shangri La after an absence of about six years—the courtyard was significantly altered. The plantings on all walls were removed and replaced with colored-glass windows. These windows were copied from an original in the foyer and set along the lower registers of the

LEFT View from the living room looking into the central courtyard, showing the stacked tile panels at the base of the stairwell, ca. 1940.

BELOW Tile panel, Iran, seventeenth century or later. Stonepaste: underglaze painted, 55 3/8 x 74 3/8 in. (140.7 x 188.9 cm). In the central courtyard.

The central courtyard, with the late
thirteenth-century Iranian tiles partially
installed and framed by a pair of
mirrored wood columns, early 1940s.

RIGHT Detail of tile panel, Iran, late thirteenth century. Stonepaste: molded, glazed and unglazed, each tile: 7 x 7 in. (17.8 x 17.8 cm). In the central courtyard.

BELOW Late-thirteenth-century Iranian tile panel, glazed and unglazed stonepaste, in the central courtyard.

east and west walls. Duke lived with this alteration for a number of years, but she must not have been entirely satisfied with it. During the 1950s and 1960s, she continued to purchase seventeenth–nineteenth-century Iranian tile panels with a very specific aesthetic.[16] The tiles she sought out had white or yellow backgrounds and complemented the existing historic tile panels in the courtyard, and further, they were either part of a matching set or else identical or corresponding in general size and color to an existing example in the collection.[17] Sometime in the late 1960s, once Duke had acquired all the additional panels she needed to create the symmetry required, she transformed the courtyard into its present appearance. Panels she had purchased that had failed to meet the necessary specifications were excluded from the final installation. For example, a tile panel of similar date and design, but with a greenish-brown background, was relegated to the Playhouse.[18] Another panel of similar design and color and size to those in the courtyard, but with no match-ing partner, was first located in the billiards room and later moved to the staff hall, where it is memorably installed on its side to suit the sight line into the hall. After more than thirty years of struggle, Doris Duke had attained an aesthetic for the courtyard that she found satisfactory. With art, architecture, and landscape in harmony, renovations to the courtyard ended and Duke's collecting of seventeenth–nineteenth-century Iranian tiles likewise ended.

The distinct relationship that exists at Shangri La between building, landscape, and collection cannot be fully understood by walking around the estate today. The

LEFT The central courtyard as seen today with tile panels below and colored-glass windows along the walls' upper registers. The court's central landscaping includes a shower tree.

ABOVE The central courtyard, showing colored-glass windows along the east wall's lower register, ca. 1946.

ABOVE Tile panel, Iran, seventeenth century. Stonepaste:
underglaze painted, 55 9/16 x 36 7/8 in. (131.1 x 93.7 cm).
In the ladies' hall in the Playhouse.

RIGHT Tile panel without a matching partner set at the
far end of the hallway to the staff wing. See page 129.

relationship developed over decades in a gradual process, the history of which has been partially erased by now. But that history is captured and preserved in archival documents, which show massive tile panels being moved around the estate with apparent regularity and ease, although the reality of de-installing and re-installing them was surely a challenge. The enormity of such undertakings puts the focus sharply on art, yet an in-depth examination shows that throughout Duke's long engagement with the property, a delicate balance between art and architecture especially, but also landscape, evolved and remained true to its owner's original vision.

The two approaches Duke employed to furnish a house and build a collection of art came together in what would become her final installation. Near the end of her life, Duke, who enjoyed viewing her collection, requested that her staff bring tiles out of storage and place them in a visually integrated arrangement around the library doors. Tiles of similar color and shape were selected to make a symmetrical arrangement, filling the unadorned wall. Tiles that had been purchased for their individual merits now became part of a holistic architectural environmental. For the upper left section of the arrangement, however, no corresponding tile was available to mirror its counterpart on the right. Duke told her staff that she would complete the installation when she next visited by bringing back just the right tile. She never returned to Shangri La, and the installation remains incomplete to this day with a hole in the wall still waiting for the tile of Duke's choosing.[19]

To walk around Shangri La is to sense, whether viscerally or consciously, the presence of its founder. Shangri La is a highly personal space. The decisions about what to collect and where to display it were categorically Doris Duke's own, and as a result the site echoes her style, her creativity, and her persistence in shaping her environment. What may be less obvious to visitors is the wholesale passion Duke had for thinking about how to display Islamic art. Archival photographs reveal Duke's passion not just for collecting art, but also for situating it in ways that showcased its beauty, revealed unexpected visual relationships, and articulated its characteristics within the site's context in Honolulu. In addition to the examples discussed here, a host of objects came to have a symbiotic relationship with Shangri La's architecture: the tent panels and chandelier in the dining room, the Syrian and Damascus Rooms, the Veramin mihrab and other luster tiles in the Mihrab Room, and the ceilings in the Playhouse are all vivid examples of this evolving relationship. Her strategies of site-specific collecting for design came together in a complementary pattern that unfolded over the course of decades, and the final result is a work of art in and of itself, true to its creator's vision.

Stairway leading to the Mughal Garden, 1941.

The mosaic tile panel shown here, commissioned
in Iran in 1938, was later re-installed on the east
wall of the dining room. where it can be seen today.

ISLAMIC ART
SELECTED OBJECTS FROM SHANGRI LA

Despite her renown, Doris Duke's achievements as a collector of Islamic art remain largely unknown. Duke never made explicit why she collected, and she never sought to gain press or social prestige through her acquisitions. While this book and the exhibition it accompanies explore Shangri La as a synthesis of architecture, landscape, and Islamic art, this portfolio offers selected highlights of Duke's holdings that are featured in the exhibition. Duke launched her efforts in 1935 with artifacts she purchased on her around-the-world honeymoon, and she continued to collect until her death in 1993. She purchased both religious and secular items rendered in a wide variety of media, emphasizing their aesthetic qualities and their cultural significance. Artifacts came from across the Islamic world, from Spain to Turkey, Iran to India. The objects featured also cover a vast time range, from a gold, pre-Islamic Persian jug dating to the first millennium BC, to late-nineteenth-century Indian jewelry. Duke's collecting extended beyond historic material to commissions, including the lunette shown here that was part of a larger tile panel custom made in the late 1930s for Shangri La by an Iranian tile workshop. Working on every scale from jewelry to architectural elements, Duke was always drawn to the rich materials and intricate decorative patterning of Islamic art traditions. This portfolio underscores the reach of Duke's lifelong travels, interests, and discerning eye.

PAGE 134 Doris Duke at Shangri La, 1966.

ABOVE Covered bowl, Northern India,
nineteenth century. Rock crystal, gold, silver,
and gemstones, 2 1/4 x 3 3/16 in. (5.7 x 8.1 cm).

LEFT Rosewater sprinkler, Northern India,
eighteenth century. Enameled gold
and gemstones, 9 x 3 3/4 in. (24.1 x 9.5 cm).

RIGHT Woman with a Cat, Iran, late eighteenth
century. Oil on canvas, 64 1/2 x 34 3/4 in.
(163.8 x 88.3 cm).

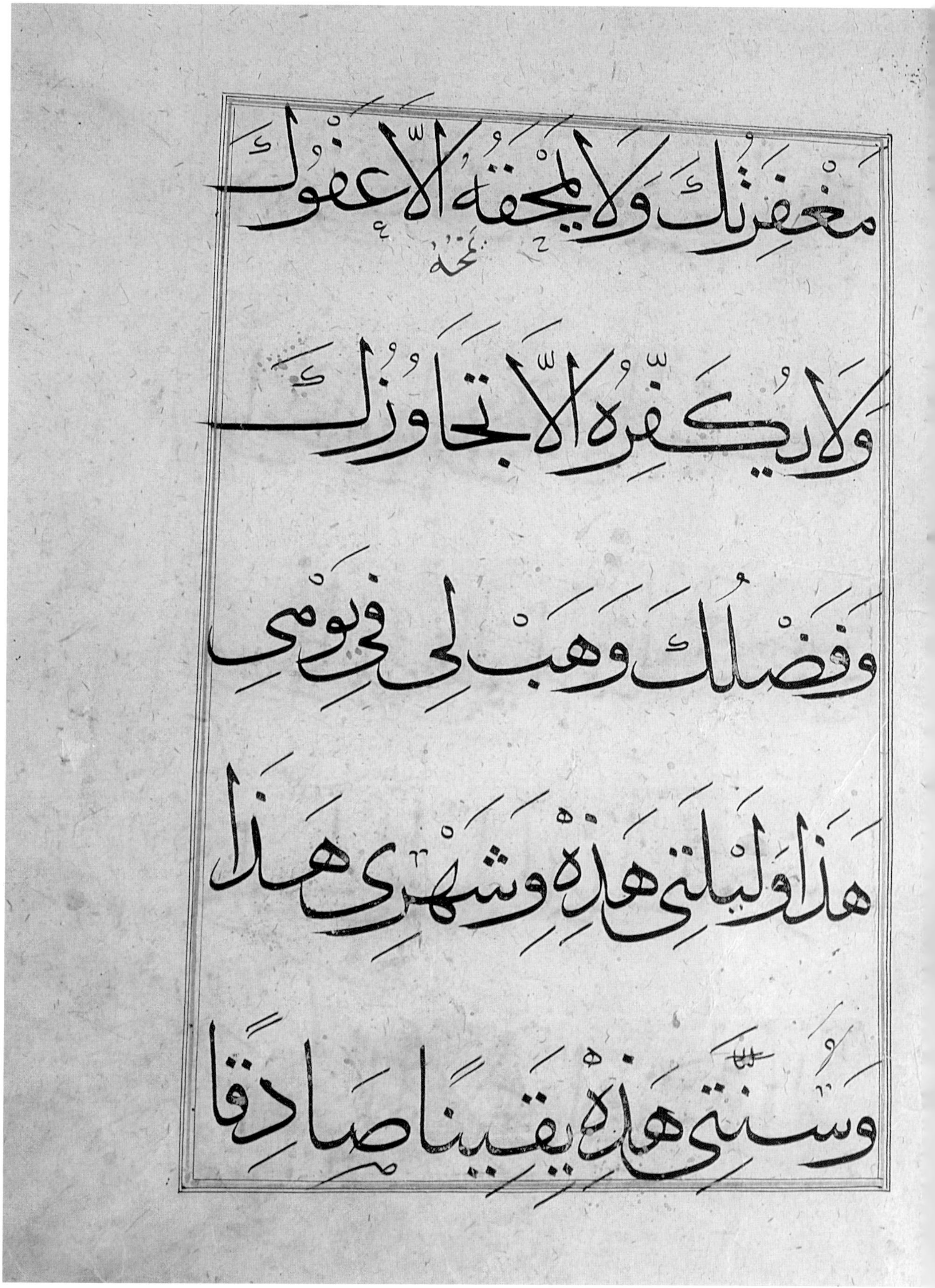
مغفرتك ولا يمحقه الا عفوك
يمحقه
ولا يكفره الا تجاوزك
وفضلك وهب لي في يومي
هذا وليلتي هذه وشهري هذا
وسنتي هذه يقينا صادقا

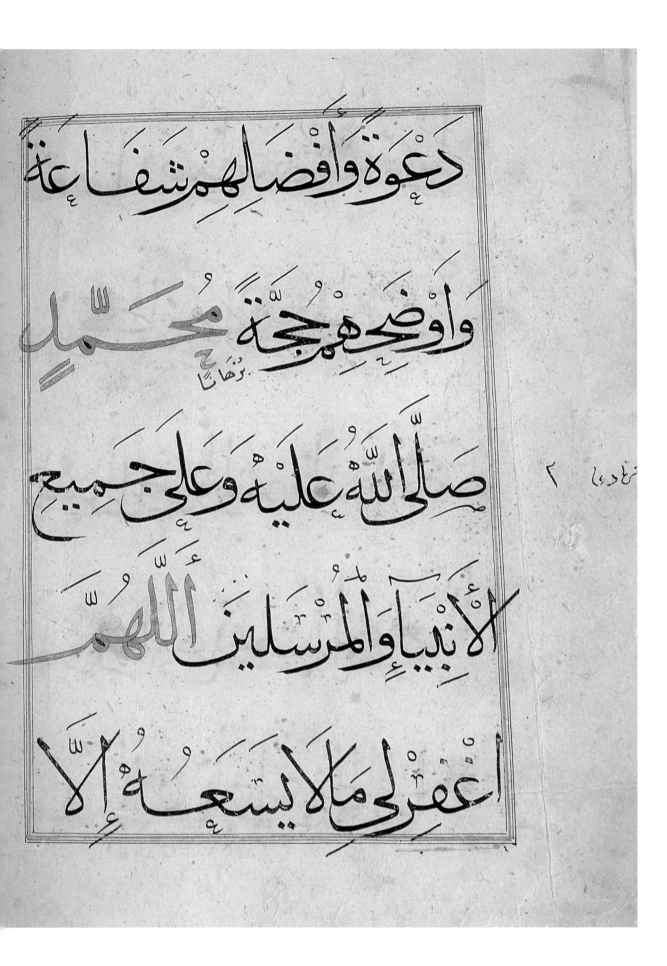

دَعْوَةً وَأَفْضَلُهُمْ شَفَاعَةً

وَأَوْضَحُهُمْ حُجَّةً مُحَمَّد

صَلَّى اللهُ عَلَيْهِ وَعَلَى جَمِيعِ

الْأَنْبِيَاءِ وَالْمُرْسَلِينَ اللَّهُمَّ

اغْفِرْ لِي مَا لَا يَسَعُهُ إِلَّا

Manuscript of religious
devotions, North Africa,
dated AH 886/1481–82
AD. Ink and gold on
paper with gilded-leather
binding, 11 3/4 x 8 1/2 in.
(29.8 x 21.6 cm).

ABOVE Footed basin, Spain, Valencia, probably
Manises, ca. 1500. Earthenware: underglaze
painted in blue, overglaze painted in luster,
7 1/8 x 10 in. (18.1 x 25.4 cm).

LEFT Dish, Turkey, Iznik, ca. 1580–85. Stonepaste with underglaze painting, diameter:
10 1/2 in. (26.7 cm).

RIGHT Dish, Spain, Valencia, probably Manises,
ca. 1470–1500. Earthenware: molded, overglaze
painted in luster, diameter: 13 3/4 in. (34.9 cm).

LEFT North wall of the living room with a thirteenth-century Spanish fireplace flanked by fifteenth–sixteenth century Spanish luster chargers.

RIGHT Tile panel, Turkey, possibly Istanbul, ca. 1650. Stonepaste: underglaze painted, 44 x 10 1/2 in. (111.8 x 26.7 cm).

ABOVE Bowl, Iran, probably Kashan, early
thirteenth century. Stonepaste: molded, monochrome-glazed, 3 5/16 x 8 1/8 in. (8.4 x 20.6 cm)

RIGHT Base of a *ghalian* (water pipe), Iran,
mid-to-late seventeenth century. Stonepaste:
underglaze painted in turquoise, overglaze
painted in luster, 8 1/16 x 6 3/8 in. (20.5 x 16.2 cm).

Table, possibly Italy (Venice) or India (Goa), seventeenth–eighteenth century. Wood, mother-of-pearl, and ivory, 30 1/2 x 39 3/4 x 25 in. (77.5 x 101 x 63.5 cm). Detail at right.

BELOW Basin, Iran, probably Tabriz, late nineteenth century, endowed as waqf to the Rustamiyya mosque at the shrine of Sayyid Hamza in the Surkhab quarter of Tabriz in AH 1291/1874 AD. Engraved tinned copper alloy, 13 1/4 x 30 1/4 in. (33.7 x 76.8 cm).

RIGHT Kursi (Qur'an stand), Egypt, Cairo, ca. 1900. Brass with silver and copper inlay, 33 7/8 x 18 1/2 x 18 1/2 in. (86 x 47 x 47 cm).

Chest, Syria, eighteenth–nineteenth century. Wood, mother-of-pearl, and metal fill, 36 1/8 x 56 5/8 x 24 1/8 in. (91.8 x 143.8 x 61.3 cm).

ABOVE Bracelet, India, late seventeenth–early eighteenth century. Enameled gold with rubies and diamonds, 4 1/2 x 9 in. (11.4 x 22.9 cm).

RIGHT *Jhabbedar* (pair of ear ornaments), India, Delhi, nineteenth century. Enameled gold with white sapphires, rubies, seed pearls, emerald beads, length: 9 1/2 in. (24.1 cm).

LEFT Bindalli (wedding dress), Turkey, late nineteenth–early twentieth century. Silk velvet with cotton and metallic threads, 54 x 18 in. (137.2 x 45.7 cm).

RIGHT Carpet, Turkey, nineteenth century. Silk, 50 x 70 in. (127 x 177.8 cm).

153

ABOVE Hand mirror, Northern India, nineteenth century. Jade, gold, gemstones, and mica, diameter: 9 1/8 in. (23.2 cm).

LEFT Jug, Iran, early first millennium BC. Gold, 7 3/8 x 3 1/2 in. (18.7 x 8.9 cm).

RIGHT Necklace, India, late nineteenth–early twentieth century. Enameled gold with cabochon rubies, diamonds, and silk cord, 6 5/16 x 18 11/16 in. (16 x 47.5 cm). View of front.

156

LEFT Necklace seen on previous page.
View of back.

ABOVE Pair of bracelets, India, Jaipur,
ca. 1900. Enameled gold with rubies and
diamonds, diameter: 2 15/16 in. (7.5 cm).

RIGHT Box with cover, Northern India,
late nineteenth century. Enameled gold,
1 3/4 x 2 1/2 in. (4.4 x 6.4 cm).

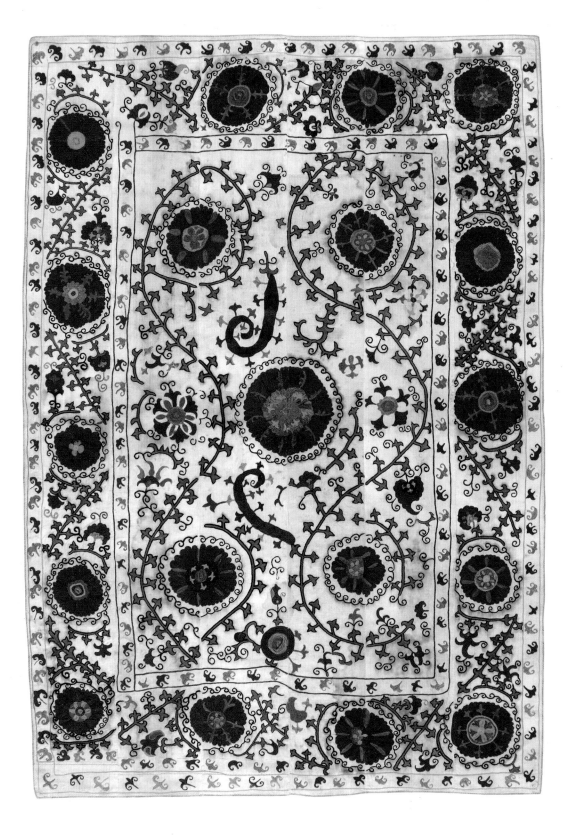

LEFT Doris Duke and Sam Kahanamoku
playing guitars at Shangri La, 1939.

ABOVE Suzani, Uzbekistan, Bukhara region,
late nineteenth century. Cotton with silk
threads, 102 1/2 x 67 1/2 in. (260.4 x 171.5 cm).

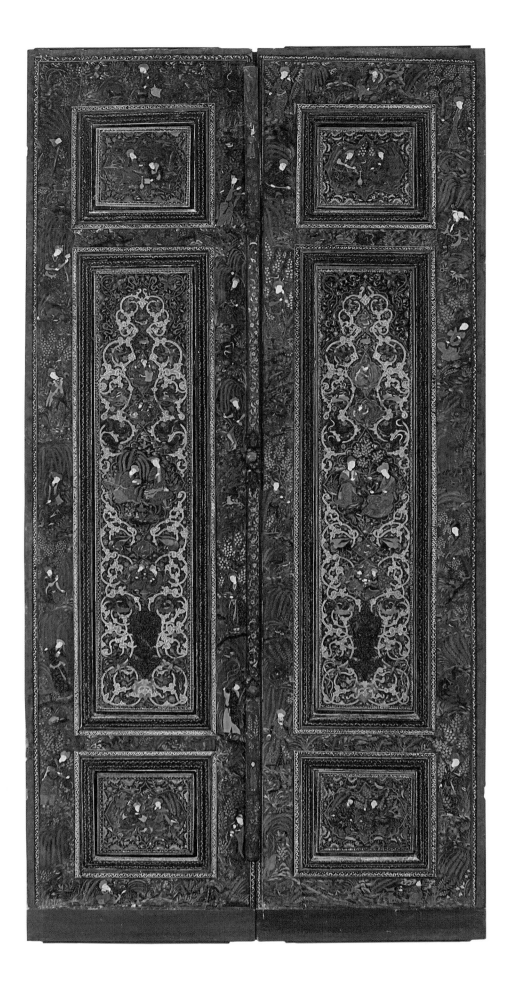

FAR LEFT Pair of doors, Iran, late nineteenth century. Wood, pigments, varnish, and metal hardware, 77 1/2 x 19 3/4 x 1 3/4 in. (196.9 x 50.2 x 4.4 cm).

ABOVE Ceiling lamp, Syria, Damascus, twentieth century. Cast, pierced, and engraved brass, 19 1/2 x 13 in. (49.5 x 33.0 cm).

LEFT Floor lamp, Egypt or Syria, ca. 1900. Copper alloy, 60 1/2 x 20 3/16 in. (153.7 x 51.3 cm).

ABOVE Bottle with depictions of dance and
music themes, Iran, probably Isfahan, early-to-mid
seventeenth century. Stonepaste: molded,
monochrome-glazed, 9 1/4 x 6 9/16 x 3 7/8 in.
(23.5 x 16.7 x 9.8 cm).

RIGHT Rosewater sprinkler, Iran, eighteenth–
nineteenth century. Mold-blown and free-blown
glass, 15 3/8 x 5 in. (39.1 x 12.7 cm).

FAR RIGHT Detail of floor lamp, Egypt or Syria, late
nineteenth century. Copper alloy, 68 x 21 1/2 in.
(172.7 x 54.6 cm). Decorating the wall behind is a
panel of star and cross tiles, Iran, late nineteenth
century. Stonepaste: molded, underglaze painted,
each tile: 7 3/4 x 7 3/4 in. (19.7 x 19.7 cm).

LEFT Central courtyard hanging lamp.

ABOVE Lunette, formerly part of the mosaic panel currently on view in the dining room. Custom-made for Shangri La by a workshop in Isfahan, Iran, in 1938–39. Stonepaste: monochrome-glazed, assembled as mosaic, 12 x 23 1/4 in. (30.5 x 59.1 cm).

TOP LEFT Star tile with phoenix, Iran, early fourteenth century. Stonepaste: underglaze painted in cobalt blue, overglaze painted in luster, 3/4 x 8 x 5/8 in. (1.9 x 20.3 x 1.6 cm).

BOTTOM LEFT Star tile with phoenix, Iran, late thirteenth–early fourteenth century. Stonepaste: molded, monochrome-glazed, diameter: 8 1/8 in. (20.6 cm).

RIGHT Group of star and cross tiles, Iran, thirteenth–fourteenth century. Stonepaste: some molded, monochrome-glazed; some underglaze painted in blue, overglaze painted in luster. In the Mihrab Room.

ABOVE Bottle with portraits of Qajar rulers, made in Bohemia for the Iranian market, nineteenth century. Colored glass, beads, and image transfer (portraits), 6 1/8 x 3 1/4 x 2 3/4 in. (15.6 x 8.3 x 7 cm).

RIGHT Tent panel with Qur'anic inscription, Egypt, Cairo, nineteenth century. Cotton appliqué, 153 x 68 1/2 in. (388.6 x 174 cm).

Chair, Iran, early nineteenth century.
Wood, ivory, ebony, and metal
hardware, 46 3/8 x 24 1/4 x 26 1/4 in.
(117.8 x 61.6 x 66.7 cm). Detail at left.

ABOVE Ewer, Iran, late eighteenth–nineteenth century. Mold-blown and free-blown glass, 6 1/2 x 5 1/4 in. (16.5 x 13.3 cm).

LEFT Ewer, Kashmir, late nineteenth–early twentieth century. Silver, 6 1/2 x 7 13/16 x 4 7/8 in. (16.5 x 19.8 x 12.4 cm).

RIGHT Pair of doors, Northern India, nineteenth century. Wood, ivory, enamel, pigments, mica, and metal hardware, 84 3/4 x 22 1/2 x 5 in. (215.3 x 57.2 x 12.7 cm).

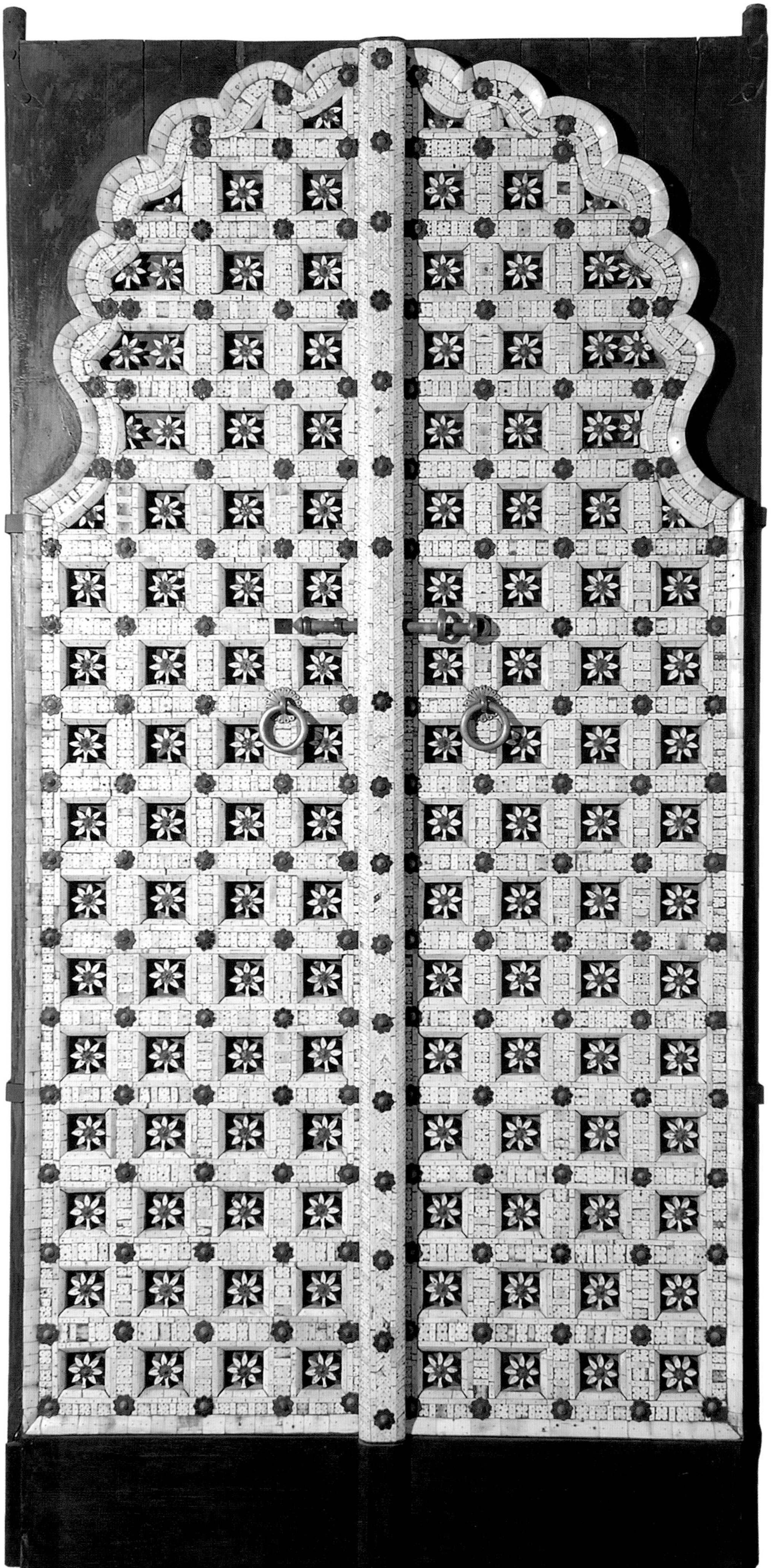

INVENTIVE SYNTHESIS
THE ARCHITECTURE AND DESIGN OF SHANGRI LA

Thomas Mellins and Donald Albrecht

Begun in 1936, Doris Duke's aptly named Shangri La, a five-acre Honolulu estate overlooking the Pacific Ocean, may initially seem to be the architectural product of an heiress pursuing her own highly eccentric ideal of a remote and exotic dream house. Located approximately two thousand five hundred miles from the American mainland in what was then a territory of the United States, Shangri La was both geographically and socially distant from the wealthy enclaves of Palm Beach and Newport, which Duke and her circle had chosen for retreat. Shangri La, with its heady infusion of Islamic art and architectural references, also seems stylistically out of character for Duke, the daughter of a Gilded Age titan, raised as she was in a Beaux Arts mansion on Manhattan's Fifth Avenue. Yet, in conceiving and implementing plans for Shangri La, Duke was no dilettante. Over many decades, she pursued a deep interest in the arts and cultures of the Islamic world, taking extensive travels, consulting with a broad network of individuals from scholars to dealers, and far exceeding the concerns of someone seeking only to decorate a hideaway.

In designing the house, Duke worked with architects and designers who, building on their classical Western educations, felt comfortable adopting the

PAGE 174 Dining room at Shangri La
as redecorated by Doris Duke in the 1960s.

RIGHT Early rendering of Shangri La's
front entrance, ca. 1936.

BELOW Early rendering of Shangri La as
seen from the ocean, July 28, 1936.

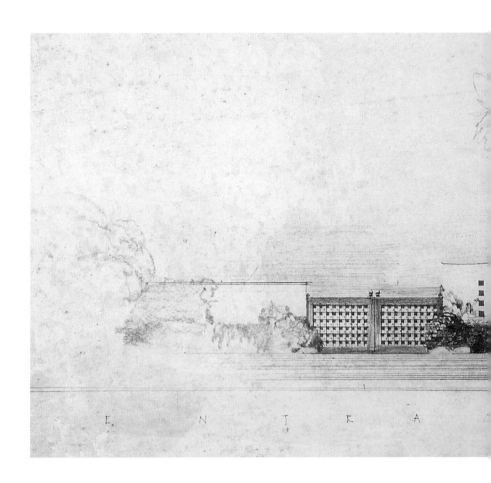

artistic traditions of non-Western cultures and marrying them to contemporary aesthetic trends, social conditions, and technological innovations. The estate, for which Marion Sims Wyeth (1889–1992) served as principal architect, features a fourteen-thousand-square-foot main house, with allusions — some general and some specific — to architectural landmarks from the ancient city of Persepolis to those of the Islamic period, such as the Alhambra and the Taj Mahal. Shangri La also encompasses a dining room enclosed in floor-to-ceiling glass walls; a play-house pavilion inspired by the seventeenth-century Chihil Sutun in Isfahan; a swimming pool equipped with an ultramodern, hydraulically controlled diving board; courtyards; and a Mughal-style garden carved out of the lush natural sur-roundings of Hawai'i.

Building Shangri La and assembling the Islamic art collections it houses, Duke pursued neither an encyclopedic approach nor one based solely on connois-seurship. Shangri La powerfully demonstrates eclecticism, perhaps best described as "inventive synthesis." Duke's extensive collections reflect her far-ranging inter-ests in objects from different parts of the Islamic world — from Spain to the Philippines — as well as from different time periods, ranging from the eighth to the

ABOVE Early aerial perspective of Shangri La, ca. 1936. The wide staircase leading to the shoreline and the terraces and other sea-level structures were never built.

RIGHT Early drawing of Shangri La, looking toward the living and dining rooms, 1936–39. The massive staircase leading to the shoreline was never built.

Drawing of a scheme for Shangri La's
foyer by P. Vary of S.A.L.A.M. Réne Martin,
Rabat, Morocco, May 1937.

twentieth centuries. Duke also wove together original and commissioned pieces. Rather than diminish the results of her efforts, this aesthetic freedom is now considered one of the hallmarks of the house she created and the collections she amassed. For example, the holdings are of increasing interest to scholars today because Duke was drawn to things that few contemporaneous collectors or museums acquired, such as nineteenth-century Qajar paintings from Persia.

The concept of inventive synthesis can be seen throughout Shangri La. Complete historic rooms, sometimes modified to fit the dimensions of specific spaces, function as museum-quality period installations, while in other spaces, Duke commissioned contemporary artisans to create architectural and decorative elements utilizing traditional forms, patterns, and means of fabrication. In the living room, the contrast between the ornately decorated Moroccan ceiling and the adjacent glass wall that fully retracts into the basement, as well as the juxtaposition of medieval ceramics with modern drapery and upholstery textiles by the designer Dorothy Liebes, epitomize Duke's approach.

Just as Duke's aesthetic sensibility was eclectic, so, too, was the mix of people with whom she worked, from antique dealers in Damascus and Venice to department-store retailers in New York. In addition to Wyeth, Duke hired Rabat-based René Martin to oversee the creation of Moroccan architectural features for several Shangri La interiors, and she was advised by Arthur Upham Pope, a controversial and internationally known figure in Islamic art scholarship and collecting. Pope introduced Duke to Ayoub Rabenou, of Tehran and Paris, from whom she purchased antique objects and commissioned new mosaic and underglaze tile panels. It seems likely that Pope was also responsible for introducing Duke to the Damascus-based firm of Asfar & Sarkis. In New York, Duke purchased from H. Khan Monif and made acquisitions from William Randolph Hearst's collections through sales at Gimbels department store. Duke also worked with Mary Crane, a graduate student of Islamic art at New York University and a member of Pope's fieldwork team in Iran; Hagop Kevorkian, a collector and dealer; and Parke-Bernet Galleries.

The exact origins of Shangri La can be traced to February 13, 1935, when Duke married the socially prominent James H. R. Cromwell and set off on a ten-month, heavily publicized, around-the-world honeymoon. Throughout the trip, newspapers reported on the couple's comings and goings, including their chat with Mahatma Gandhi about the machine age and their visit to the Taj Mahal, which would prove to be the spark for Shangri La. "While we were in Agra Pete [Doris Duke] had fallen in love with the Taj Mahal and all the beautiful marble tile, with their [sic] lovely floral designs with some precious stones," Cromwell wrote to his mother from India, noting that this love would be realized in a bedroom-and-bathroom suite that he and Duke planned to build as part of an addition to Malmaison, his house on his mother's Palm Beach estate, El Mirasol. "Due to the India environment and cooking, plumbing was possibly the utmost thing on her mind," Cromwell continued, noting that he and Duke "went to the tile factory in Agra, where they do such work, and got all the advice. When we got back to Delhi we got hold of the best British architect — a Mr. Blomfield — and had him draw up some tentative plans and estimates."[1] Francis B. Blomfield, along with his brother, Charles George, had worked with Edwin Lutyens on the government buildings at the British colonial capital of New Delhi. Francis Blomfield's participation in what would grow into Shangri La was the first instance of Duke's reaching out to talented, credentialed architects and designers to achieve her goals. Additionally, Blomfield's design, with its emphasis on luxurious and luminous surfaces of pure-white marble inset with delicate and intricate patterns of lapis lazuli, jade, and malachite; its door and window jalis (latticed screens); and carved marble doorways presaged the aesthetic of the finished house.

In May 1935 the commission for the building in which the so-called Mughal Suite would sit went to local Palm Beach–based architect Maurice Fatio, Blomfield apparently having expressed no interest in the opportunity. Fatio was not approached by Duke or Cromwell, but rather by an ambassador: Cromwell's mother, Eva Stotesbury. Palm Beach's leading hostess, Stotesbury was also a significant architectural patron, having commissioned the architect Horace Trumbauer to design her Philadelphia estate, Whitemarsh Hall, while Addison Mizner, the architect who initiated Palm Beach's dominant Mediterranean-inspired style, designed Stotesbury's Palm Beach estate.[2] The estate encompassed a pavilion described at the time as the Moorish Teahouse; there was also a monumental gateway designed by Fatio in a complementary style.[3] Referring to her son and daughter-in-law, Stotesbury

ABOVE Postcard of El Mirasol, Addison Mizner's residence for Edward and Eva Stotesbury, Palm Beach.

LEFT Loggia of El Mirasol.

wrote to the architect, "She and Jimmy have given me carte blanche to select an architect.... Of course, in view of the exquisite Hispano Moresque you did for me at El Mirasol.... I have selected you as the only architect capable of reproducing the Taj Mahal into Palm Beach-esque!"[4]

One of the top architects to work extensively in Palm Beach, Maurice Fatio was born into a wealthy family in Geneva, Switzerland, in 1897 and attended the internationally renowned Federal Polytechnic Institute there, studying with the prolific, pioneering modernist architect Koloman Moser. Fatio came to the United States in 1920 and took a job with the architect Harrie T. Lindeberg, who specialized in the design of grand, English-inspired country estates, particularly on Long Island. Fatio later established a professional partnership with William A. Treanor, and over the course of a two-decade career, pursued a variety of architectural vocabularies, noting in 1921, "There are no traditions to follow [in the United States] if one wants to get away from the Colonial-style wooden house, and one is forced, for the Americans who don't want Modern art, to become eclectic, and to take one's inspiration from the best examples of the best periods of each European country."[5] Adopting an even broader eclecticism, Fatio's Palm Beach translation of the Taj Mahal resulted in a proposal for a freestanding building complete with turrets, domes, and minarets, while at the same time accommodating servants' quarters and a garage for Duke's many automobiles. Reputedly dubbed by locals the "Garage Mahal," the project never came to fruition; while Fatio was continuing to develop designs for Palm Beach, Duke and Cromwell were soon to make changes.[6]

In late August 1935, after having spent time in China and Japan, the Cromwells arrived at their last stop—Honolulu. Intending to stay two or three weeks at the Royal Hawaiian Hotel, they moved from there to a friend's house for four months—the longest stay at any one stop during their trip. By December of that year, Duke and Cromwell decided to abandon the Palm Beach project and instead to build a retreat in Honolulu, encompassing Blomfield's suite. On April 4, 1936, Duke bought the land on which Shangri La would be built. Perhaps the decision to change locations was Duke's way of removing herself from the glare of celebrity that had hounded her throughout the honeymoon. "Honolulu has made a hit with the Cromwells," a local newspaper noted, "because it has left them alone."[7]

The decision to build in Hawai'i also allowed Duke to distance herself from the Florida colony presided over by her society-driven mother-in-law. This effort to establish an independent identity may have motivated Duke to change architects, though she didn't stray far from the fold and selected another Palm Beach practitioner, Marion Sims Wyeth. Born in New York City in 1889 to a family of well-known physicians, Wyeth was educated at Princeton and Paris's École des Beaux Arts. As a young architect, he worked for Bertram Grosvenor Goodhue and for Carrère & Hastings. Interestingly, in light of Shangri La, Goodhue, who would design the Honolulu Academy of Arts, was well versed in Islamic architecture. He had visited Egypt, the Arabian Peninsula, and Persia in 1903 with his client J. Waldron Gillespie, for whom he designed a Montecito, California, estate, complete with Persian-style gardens.[8] In 1919 Wyeth started his own office in Palm

FAR LEFT Interior of El Mirasol.

ABOVE Maurice Fatio's entrance gate at El Mirasol.

Treanor & Fatio's rendering of an addition to Malmaison, Palm Beach, ca. 1935. Planned to house the Mughal Suite, commissioned by Doris Duke and her husband in India, this unbuilt scheme incorporated direct references to the Taj Mahal.

Rough Sketch Patio Side

Tuscany El Patio Crdt

Two views of Malmaison, the James Cromwell
residence, on the property of El Mirasol, his
mother's estate.

Wyeth & King's Colonial Revival residence for
Anson W. Hard, Brookhaven, New York, 1925.

Marion Sims Wyeth, ca. 1940.

Beach and was joined the following year by Frederic Rhinelander King, a former classmate at the École des Beaux Arts, who led the firm's New York office.[9]

Wyeth, like Mizner, Fatio, and the latter's former employer Harrie T. Linde-berg, falls within the tradition of the "society architect." For such practitioners, social connections are both an advantage, bringing in enviable commissions, and a handicap, frequently causing their work to be taken less seriously than is deserved. Despite their talent and the quality of their designs, they are often disparaged by their peers, historians, and critics because of their focus on palatial homes over public buildings. Society architects, frequently overshadowed by their clients' wealth and notoriety, tend not to develop a single, signature style, but rather to delve into many different ones, often derived from the specific environmental and architectural conditions of place. Wyeth, for example, mastered the Colonial Revival on Long Island and, in Palm Beach, Beaux Art classicism, neo-Regency, and Mediterranean Revival—"the 'Spanish itch,' because it broke out all over Florida," as he once described the style in which he most excelled.[10] Working with their clients, society architects also tend to be willing to cede total aesthetic control of a project and collaborate with interior decorators. (Wyeth's Southwood, the Louisiana-style house he designed for Dr. John A. Vietor in Palm Beach, embraced dramatic interiors by celebrated decorator Ruby Ross Wood.) At the same time, their elegant personal style and demeanor help them fit within their clients' social milieu. While these qualities help explain why Wyeth is not more widely known—there is no published monograph of his work—they also underscore why this self-effacing architect proved an ideal choice to work with the strong-willed and opinionated Doris Duke and her husband on Shangri La.

Once the Cromwells hired Wyeth, work on Shangri La proceeded quickly. Ground was broken in March 1937 with the construction of a stone seawall, which held back infill to create a stepped site. When seen from the ocean, the site and its buildings were an imposing presence; at the same time, the house was largely shielded from neighboring properties and the road above. To help with the design, Wyeth brought in a young associate, H. Drewry Baker, who had graduated from Princeton's School of Architecture. In the 1920s Baker had designed a New York City restaurant for the enterprising Alice Foote MacDougall that evoked an Italian streetscape with a small-scale reproduction of Florence's Ponte Vecchio. *The New Yorker* described it as an "indoors al fresco restaurant."[11] Baker's capacity to create scenographic architecture proved valuable in Wyeth's initial plans for Shangri La. An early design for the master bedroom suite incorporated delicately filigreed windows and railings inspired by Islamic traditions, and most strikingly, a tower resembling a minaret. While the house was under construction, the Cromwells traveled throughout Europe, including Antibes on the French Riviera, where they met up with René Martin, and upon their return to Hawai'i in the summer of 1937, showed sketches by his chief designer P. Vary to Wyeth. As in the Blomfield design for the Mughal Suite, the Moroccan workshop further realized Duke's abiding interest in sensuous surfaces incorporating geometric pattern and a complex layering of spatial experience achieved through the use of traditional screens. At the same time, Martin engaged Moroccan craftsmen who applied

LEFT The entrance hall of Wyeth & King's residence for Dr. John A. Vietor, Palm Beach, 1935. The interiors of the house were designed by New York–based decorator Ruby Ross Wood.

BELOW Vietor residence.

DONAHUE RESIDENCE, PALM BEACH, FLORIDA

LEFT Marion Sims Wyeth's residence
for Mr. and Mrs. James P. Donahue,
Palm Beach, 1927.

ABOVE Postcard of Donahue residence.

traditional craft techniques in the manufacture of elements, which included intricately carved ceilings.

As the process of designing both the exterior and the interior of the house continued, a shift in direction occurred. Wyeth, Baker, and the Cromwells synthesized their scenographic approach with a more formally neutral, modern aesthetic that they felt was sympathetic to the display of the burgeoning collections. Their abandonment of the proposed minaret and an illustrative mural depicting Isfahan, as called for in an earlier "Pan-Asian" scheme for the living room, also might have been a reaction against the theatrical qualities of such local Hawaiian projects as the Persian Room in the Royal Hawaiian Hotel or the caricatured Japanese style of C. W. Dickey's Toyo Theatre, completed in 1938.

The decision to incorporate modernism into the "inventive synthesis" apparent throughout the estate can also be seen within broader architectural trends. During the 1920s and '30s, various facets of modernism had been advanced by American architects and designers. Hallmarks of the style—asymmetrical massing, large expanses of undecorated wall, extensive glazing, and indirect lighting—influenced Shangri La and Wyeth's other buildings, and those of his Palm Beach–based colleagues. As early as 1924, for example, Mizner's Warden House featured floor-to-ceiling glass panels that fully retracted into the ground—a technology usually attributed to Ludwig Mies van der Rohe's Tugendhat House of 1930 in Brno, Czechoslovakia, and later used at Shangri La.[12] In 1934 Fatio would adopt an explicitly modernist vocabulary, with flat roofs and casement windows, for the Loening House

LEFT The courtyard of Wyeth & King's Norton Museum of Art, West Palm Beach, 1941.

ABOVE Norton Museum of Art.

·SECTION · LOOKING

Drawing dated January 15, 1937 of a
"Pan-Asian" scheme for the living
room at Shangri La, which juxtaposed
East Asian furnishings and a Chinese
sculpture with a mural of the *maidan*
(square) in Isfahan, Iran.

ABOVE Addison Mizner's residence for William Gray Warden, Palm Beach, 1922. This view shows the house's loggia, which featured windows that fully retract into the ground.

RIGHT Drawing of a scheme for the Mughal Suite at Shangri La, with a minaret-like tower, ca. 1936.

in Palm Beach. Wyeth himself adopted a modern classicism for the Norton Museum of Art in West Palm Beach, completed in 1941, as well as for a series of houses and commercial structures completed after World War II. This trend shaped many of Shangri La's forms and spaces, most strikingly its glass-walled dining room. "Contrasting with [Shangri La's] Orientalia," Duke wrote in 1947, "is the completely modern dining-room. As no Near Eastern house ever had a dining-room, it seemed foolish to try to create one."13

Yet the modern dining room at Shangri La was not to last. It was transformed by Duke herself in the 1960s into a tent-like environment, created with richly colored tent hangings and containing a chandelier made in France for export to India. Indeed, Duke continued to make changes and additions, large and small, for the rest of her life. Ironically, what began as a secluded place of rest was energized by its owner's restless imagination. Shangri La thus proves to be no mere folly; it is a house forged by twentieth-century trends in architecture and place-making, as well as by Doris Duke's own aesthetic drive and seriousness of purpose.

· SECTION · LOOKING · WEST ·

ABOVE LEFT Drawing of the dining room at
Shangri La, ca. 1935.

BELOW LEFT Drawing of the glass wall in the
living room at Shangri La, January 14, 1937.

ABOVE The dining room at Shangri La.

LEFT The dining room at Shangri La, ca. 1947.

BELOW The dining room at Shangri La as redecorated by Doris Duke in the 1960s.

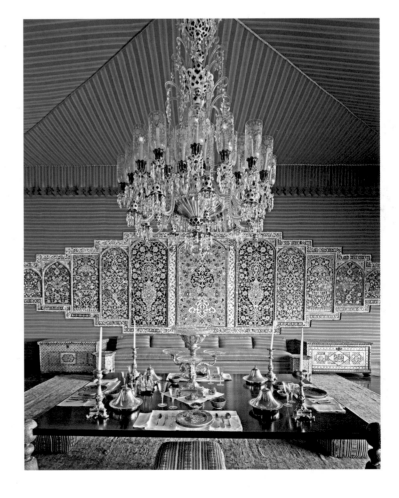

CONTEMPORARY ARTISTS RESPOND TO SHANGRI LA

Since 2004 Shangri La has hosted scholars and artists in residence whose work complements the collection and also advances the study and understanding of Islamic art and culture. Invited scholars and artists pursue their own academic and creative work and also present public programs, such as lectures, workshops, and performances. In order to bring this program to a broader audience, six former artists in residence were invited to create work that was inspired by their experiences of the site to be included in the exhibition *Doris Duke's Shangri La.*

RIGHT Afruz Amighi. *Rocket Gods,* 2010. Aluminum and base-metal chain, each of three elements 59 x 9 in. (149.9 x 22.9 cm).

FAR RIGHT AND BELOW Afruz Amighi. *Heart Axe,* 2011. Woven polyethylene and plexiglass, 96 x 68 in. (243.8 x 172.7 cm).

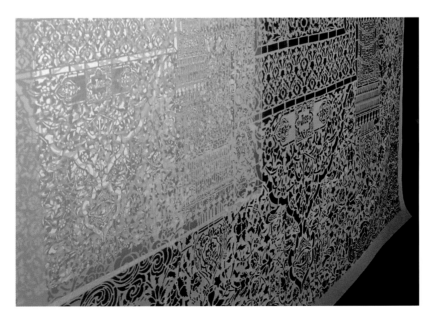

AFRUZ AMIGHI

(b. 1974)

RESIDENCY November 1–14, 2010

Cosponsored by the University of Hawai'i Department of Art and Art History

There is a hidden state within all forms. Doris Duke's Shangri La, an Islamic palace in lush, verdant Honolulu, is an idyllic Eden. Like a three-dimensional Persian carpet, it is a reminder here on earth of what awaits the faithful in paradise. But it is an oasis fringed by peril: It is surrounded by ten major military bases and installations. In 2009 US military spending topped twelve billion dollars in Hawai'i, encompassing 18 percent of total expenditures in the state. The juxtaposition of violence and opulence is the theme that dominates my work for this exhibition. Missiles and rockets rendered in aluminum and silver chain mimic chandeliers and lanterns. These forms, associated with the arms-manufacturing industry, are masked in a veneer of decadence, highlighting their function as the mainstays of wealth in our economy. The work alludes to an underlying menace, creating a realm in which violence and tranquility collide.

Shangri La is a shrine to the majesty of monumental architecture. Isfahani mihrabs, Moroccan tiles, and Syrian wood paneling form a seamless landscape that is testament to the beauty and solace found in the architecture of power. Heart Axe reflects this kaleidoscope of patterns and designs. As peacock feathers transform into pointed arrows amidst a Cairene geometric relief and chains ensnare a human heart suspended on a backdrop from the Alhambra, the overwhelming palace and mosque recede. Their monumental forms dematerialize into shadow — and illusions of power lose their stronghold. Afruz Amighi, 2011

Born in Tehran, Afruz Amighi received her BA in political science from Barnard College in 1997 and her MFA from New York University in 2007. In 2006 Amighi was selected for Emerge 7, a program for emerging artists sponsored by Aljira, a Center for Contemporary Art, in collaboration with Creative Capital. She has shown her work extensively in the United States, London, and the Middle East, and she is the recipient of the inaugural Jameel Prize, awarded by London's Victoria and Albert Museum in 2009. In 2011 Amighi received a fellowship in sculpture from the New York Foundation for the Arts. Amighi's work is in the permanent collections of the Metropolitan Museum of Art; the Victoria and Albert Museum; the Museum of Fine Arts, Houston; the Bristol Museum and Art Gallery in England; and the Devi Institute in New Delhi. Amighi lives and works in New York.

ZAKARIYA AMATAYA

(b. 1975)

RESIDENCY June 15–July 8, 2011

Cosponsored by the University of Hawai'i Outreach College

Poet Zakariya Amataya was born in Narathiwat, one of Thailand's three Muslim-majority southern provinces. He writes in four languages — Malay, Thai, Arabic, and English — and often interprets the conflicts between Muslims and Buddhists in Southeast Asia. Working in the tradition of American Beat poets such as Allen Ginsberg, he was, in 2010, Thailand's first Muslim recipient of the Southeast Asian Writers Award, the region's most important literary prize. Amataya lives and works in Bangkok.

EMRE HÜNER

(b. 1977)

RESIDENCY August 15–31, 2011
Cosponsored by the University of Hawai'i Department of Art and Art History

The architectural aspects and visual archives of Shangri La were the first elements I worked with during my residency. Exploring construction images of the property, I had the chance to learn more about Doris Duke and her personal stories that relate to the collection. I was intrigued by the eclectic character of the space. Working on a 16mm film, I sought to depict the past and capture the contemporary essence of Shangri La, including a maquette of the house and various photographs of animals, the diving board and pool, plants, and people. Tracing hidden or overlooked details, my work focuses on the filmic and sculptural qualities found in these artifacts as well as their possible narratives. Emre Hüner, 2011

Born in Istanbul, Emre Hüner is an artist who produces drawings, videos, and spatial works using different techniques. Based on an extensive archive of imagery and found materials, Hüner's work investigates the language of modernist progress and its paradoxical heritage. Attributing various meanings to the sculptural objects and drawings, from organic to architectural, artificial and naturalistic, Hüner creates and reassembles an eclectic order of layers. His recent work traces the relationship between the archaic and the futuristic, alluding, among other things, to prehistoric tools, sedimentary rocks, utopian constructions, and explorers. Hüner has had numerous exhibitions of his work worldwide, including in the Hague; Antwerp; Istanbul; Busan, South Korea; and Munich. He was also featured in the New Museum's exhibition *The Generational: Younger Than Jesus* in New York. He lives and works in Amsterdam and Istanbul.

LEFT, ABOVE, AND BELOW Emre Hüner. Studies for Untitled, 2011. Digital images.

RIGHT Mohamed Zakariya. There Is Nothing Like Him, 2005. Ink and gold on Turkish ahar paper in Jeli talik script, 23 ¼ x 12 ¼ in. (59.1 x 31.1 cm).

MOHAMED ZAKARIYA

(b. 1942)

RESIDENCY September 7–28, 2005

When I was an artist in residence at Shangri La, my first and deepest impression was of the Pacific Ocean—the salt that corroded my steel tools, the energy and vastness of the waves breaking almost in my studio windows. The crash and roll of it, the eternity of it, the fragility of it—all this hit me after I had been there a short while. The way Shangri La rests on the volcanic earth, surrounded by palm and mango trees and over-looking the sea, evoked a Qur'anic landscape/seascape. So my choices for both works were Qur'anic.

The first piece, There is Nothing like Him, was written on a crashing high-sea afternoon in Hawai'i and finished in Virginia, using colors that came from my memory of Shangri La, and a simple gold ornament. It is on Turkish paper in Jeli talik script.

The text I chose for a second piece, which is being designed at the time of this writing, is Ayet 7 from Sura 11, Hud: "And His throne was upon the water." Although there is speculation as to its meaning, the verse has obvious Biblical echoes. Its watery connotations and creation references, however, made me think of volcanic Hawai'i. This piece will be written in the Jeli sulus script, in gold leaf, with letters approximately four to five feet high, on a synthetic canvas with background colors that remind me of Shangri La and my time there. Mohamed Zakariya, 2011

Born in California, Mohamed Zakariya—calligrapher, wood turn-er, and metalworker—combines classical standards with a mod-ern sensibility to produce works on paper and in wood. Zakariya also re-creates historic scientific instruments. Zakariya began his studies of Islam and Arabic in the 1960s and earned two licenses in Islamic calligraphy from Istanbul's Research Centre for Islamic Art, History and Culture—the first Westerner to do so. Known for his design of the "Eid Greetings" US postage stamps in 2001 and 2011, he concentrates primarily on classical Arabic and Otto-man Turkish calligraphy. Zakariya has had solo exhibitions at the Museum of Islamic Art, Doha, Qatar; Masterworks Institute for Works on Paper, San Francisco; the Bellevue Arts Museum, Washington; and the Asia Society, New York, as well as group exhi-bitions in Saudi Arabia, Dubai, and Kuwait. Zakariya lives and works in Arlington, Virginia.

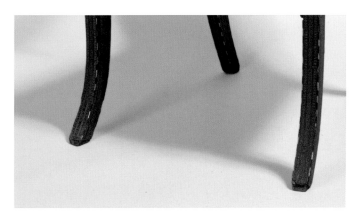

WALID RAAD

(b. 1967)

RESIDENCY October 1–25, 2009

Cosponsored by the University of Hawai'i Department of Art and Art History

I was recently taken aback by how artifacts from the Doris Duke collection of Islamic art lacked some (but not all) shadows and reflections. I decided to provide some with my work titled Preface to the Second Edition: Untitled. I am hoping that my shadows and reflections will not behave in unexpected ways.

Preface to the Second Edition: Untitled complements my ongoing project Scratching on Things I Could Disavow on the history of Arab and Islamic arts. My overall project investigates how some artifacts were affected materially and immaterially by various wars waged in Arab and Islamic lands in the past few centuries. Scratching on Things I Could Disavow also considers the emergence of a large new infrastructure for the arts in the Arabian Gulf; stories, experiences, forms, and gestures from the history of art in Lebanon; and Jalal Toufic's concept of "the withdrawal of tradition past a surpassing disaster." I would like to introduce my contribution to Doris Duke's Shangri La with the following passage from Toufic:

> With regard to the surpassing disaster, art acts like the mirror in vampire films: It reveals the withdrawal of what we think is still there. "You have seen nothing in Hiroshima" ([Marguerite] Duras's Hiroshima mon amour, 1961). Does this entail that one should not record? No. One should record this "nothing," which only after the resurrection can be available. We have to take photographs even though because of their referents' withdrawal, and until their referents are resurrected, they are not going to be available as referential,

documentary pieces—with the concomitant risk that facets relating to the subject matter might be mistaken for purely formal ones. A vicious circle: What has to be recorded has been withdrawn, so that, unless it is resurrected, it is going to be overlooked; but in order to accomplish that prerequisite work of resurrection to avert its overlooking, one has initially to have, however minimally, perceived it, that is countered its withdrawal, that is, resurrected it.[1] Walid Raad, 2012

Born in Lebanon, Walid Raad is an associate professor of art at the Cooper Union in New York. His artworks include The Atlas Group, a fifteen-year project (executed between 1989 and 2004) that explores the contemporary history of Lebanon and the ongoing projects Scratching on Things I Could Disavow: A History of Art in the Arab World and Sweet Talk: Commissions (Beirut). His books include The Truth Will Be Known When the Last Witness Is Dead; My Neck Is Thinner than a Hair; Let's Be Honest; The Weather Helped; and Scratching on Things I Could Disavow. Raad's works have been shown at Kunsthalle Zürich; Whitechapel Gallery, London; the Festival d'Automne, Paris; the Kunstenfestivaldesarts, Brussels; Documenta, Kassel; the Venice Biennale; the Hamburger Bahnhof, Berlin; and Home Works, Beirut. Raad is the recipient of the Hasselblad Award (2011), a Guggenheim Fellowship (2009), the Alpert Award in the Arts (2007), the Deutsche Börse Photography Prize (2007), and the Camera Austria Award (2005).

SHAHZIA SIKANDER

(b. 1969)

RESIDENCY November 14–30, 2008
Cosponsored by the University of Hawaiʻi Department of Art and Art History

The large-scale projections done at night were an attempt to engage with the site itself. My ongoing interest in the colonial history of the subcontinent functioned as a portal into the space. Some of the projections work as framing devices that expose elements of the landscape that are hidden at night while also extending the architecture itself. Like the wall of the living room that descends to open the house to the environment, the projections erect an invisible wall that rises high above the architecture, "hoisted" by the density of the trees. While transforming the space, the projections also recontextualize my own images by shifting the scale of the drawings and re-rendering them in foliage and architecture. Abstract, representational, and textual forms coexist and jostle for domination. Light and shadow take center stage, highlighting the textures, colors, and geometry of the space in a theater of light; evolving into a dimension that is sculptural, illusionistic, and temporary; and fleeting like the movement of wind and stars captured in the slow exposures.

Imagining Doris Duke was how I grasped the stunning site. Her presence was everywhere, permeating her collections, her house, and its extension into nature. The projection of the multi-armed female form is a metaphor for Doris Duke herself: mythical, majestic, monumental, rising from the Mughal Suite, looming over Shangri La, overlooking the formidable Pacific Ocean, where her ashes were sprinkled. The paradox of Shangri La is omnipresent. With its American orientalism, stunning craftwork, and collections from many Muslim cultures, it is engaging yet full of contradiction. Shahzia Sikander, 2011

Shahzia Sikander was educated at the National College of Arts, Lahore, Pakistan, and the Rhode Island School of Design. In the 1990s her work re-contextualized Indo-Persian miniature painting, inspiring many others to examine this tradition. The 2006 MacArthur Fellow has had recent solo exhibitions at San Francisco Art Institute; Cooper-Hewitt National Design Museum; IKON Gallery, Birmingham; Daadgalerie, Berlin; Museum of Contemporary Art, Sydney; and Irish Museum of Modern Art. Her work has been shown in numerous group exhibitions and biennials from New York to Shanghai.

LEFT Walid Raad. Untitled 1,2,3. Shadows, variable dimensions, 2012.

RIGHT Shahzia Sikander. Unseen 3 (ABOVE) and Unseen 2 (BELOW), 2011. HD-digital projections, variable dimensions.

FOLLOWING PAGE Central courtyard.

ENDNOTES

FOREWORD

1. The spelling of Hawaiian words in this book is consistent with *Hawaiian Dictionary* by Mary Kawena Pukui and Samuel H. Elbert, published by the University of Hawai'i Press in 1986.

DORIS DUKE AND THE ISLAMIC ART COLLECTING TRADITION

1. On the phenomenon of art collecting, see, for example, Joseph Alsop, *The Rare Art Traditions: The History of Art Collecting and Its Linked Phenomena Wherever Those Have Appeared* (New York: Harper & Row, 1982), in which the history of art collecting is characterized as a "social habit," xv.

2. The general details of the Duke family's history, its properties, and the life of Doris Duke are available from a variety of sources, including archival and other materials kept at Shangri La. Much of this same information is summarized in Sharon Littlefield, *Doris Duke's Shangri La* (Honolulu: Honolulu Academy of Arts and Doris Duke Foundation for Islamic Art, 2002), 3ff.

3. "Doris Duke Feted at Newport Dance," *New York Times*, August 24, 1930, in which it is noted that Duke was presented before six hundred guests.

4. See "Doris Duke at 21 Is Wealthiest Girl," *New York Times*, November 22, 1933.

5. "Doris Duke Is Wed to J.H.R. Cromwell; 'Wealthiest Girl in the World,' 22, Is Bride of Advertising Man at Surprise Ceremony," *New York Times*, February 14, 1935.

6. Littlefield, *Doris Duke's Shangri La*, 5–8.

7. See several articles in a special volume of Ars Orientalis 30 (2000): Linda Komaroff, "Exhibiting the Middle East: Collections and Perceptions of Islamic Art," 5–7; and especially Marilyn Jenkins-Madina, "Collecting the 'Orient' at the Met: Early Tastemakers in America," 69ff. and Marianna Shreve Simpson, "'A Gallant Era': Henry Walters, Islamic Art, and the Kelekian Connection," 91ff.

8. "The Edward C. Moore Collection," *The Collector* 3, no. 13 (May 1, 1892): 199–201; Jenkins-Madina, "Collecting the 'Orient' at the Met: Early Tastemakers in America," 76–80; Maryam Ekhtiar, Priscilla P. Souck, Sheila R. Canby, and Navina Najat Haidar, eds., *Masterpieces from the Department of Islamic Art in the Metropolitan Museum of Art* (New York: Metropolitan Museum of Art, 2011), 2–3 and fig. 2.

9. "The Edward C. Moore Collection."

10. Jenkins-Madina, "Collecting the 'Orient' at the Met: Early Tastemakers in America," 78–79.

11. Ibid., 79.

12. "The Edward C. Moore Collection," 199; Jenkins-Madina, "Collecting the 'Orient' at the Met: Early Tastemakers in America," 79.

13. Thomas Lawton and Linda Merrill, *Freer: A Legacy of Art*, (Washington, DC: Freer Gallery of Art, Smithsonian Institution, 1993), 13ff.

14. Ibid., 31ff.

15. On Raqqa ware in general, see Jenkins-Madina, *Raqqa Revisited: Ceramics of Ayyubid Syria* (New York: Metropolitan Museum of Art, 2006), and especially 26–27 with reference to Freer.

16. Lawton and Merrill, *Freer: A Legacy of Art*, 75, which cites Freer's letter to his business partner, Frank Hecker. On Freer's trip and the acquisitions he made in Syria, see Jenkins-Madina, *Raqqa Revisited*, 26–27.

17. Lawton and Merrill, *Freer: A Legacy of Art*, 111–14. See also Jenkins-Madina, *Raqqa Revisited*, 17–18.

18. Jenkins-Madina, "Collecting the 'Orient' at the Met: Early Tastemakers in America," 72–76. See also Stephen Vernoit, *Discovering Islamic Art: Scholars, Collectors and Collections, 1850–1950* (London: I. B. Taurus, 2000), 31.

19. Lawton and Merrill, *Freer: A Legacy of Art*, 28–29.

20. Ibid., 235ff.

21. Ibid., 9 and 200. Freer also stipulated that only works from the collection could be shown in the building; he did, nonetheless, provide a bequest for future acquisitions as a codicil to his will shortly before his death. For the specific terms of Freer's will and the codicil, see Smithsonian Institution, *Material Papers Relating to the Freer Gift and Bequest*, publication 2958 (Washington, DC: Smithsonian Institution, February 8, 1928), 1, 14.

22. William R. Johnston, *William and Henry Walters: The Reticent Collectors* (Baltimore: Johns Hopkins University Press, 1999). Also and more specifically, see Simpson, "'A Gallant Era': Henry Walters, Islamic Art, and the Kelekian Connection," 91ff.

23. Alice Cooney Frelinghuysen, Gary Tinterow, Susan Alyson Stein, Gretchen Wold, and Julia Meech, *Splendid Legacy: The Hayemeyer Collection* (New York: Metropolitan Museum of Art, 1993), 3ff.

24. Ibid., 99ff.

25. Ibid., 129ff.

26. Ibid., 130.

27. Ibid., 173ff. The interiors were designed by Louis Comfort Tiffany and Samuel Colman.

28. Ibid., 184.

29. Ibid., 177–79.

30. Ibid., 107ff.; see also Jenkins-Madina, "Collecting the 'Orient' at the Met: Early Tastemakers in America," 84–85.

31. Frelinghuysen, et al., *Splendid Legacy*, 108–109; Jenkins-Madina, "Collecting the 'Orient' at the Met: Early Tastemakers in America," 85.

32. Frelinghuysen et al., *Splendid Legacy*, 110; Jenkins-Madina, "Collecting the 'Orient' at the Met: Early Tastemakers in America," 85–86. Also, for the examples bequeathed by Horace Havemeyer, see Jenkins-Madina, *Raqqa Revisited*, 124ff.

33. See Vernoit, *Discovering Islamic Art*, 47–48.

34. See Cynthia Saltzman, *Old Masters, New World: America's Raid on Europe's Great Pictures 1880–World War I* (New York: Viking, 2008), among the most recent of a number of books on this subject, which mainly focus on European art.

35. Frelinghuysen et al., *Splendid Legacy*, 197.

36. Ekhtiar et al., *Masterpieces from the Department of Islamic Art in the Metropolitan Museum of Art*, 2–4.

37. "Doris Duke and the Newport Restoration Foundation Timeline," compiled by Bruce MacLeish [accessed at Shangri La on July 29, 2011]. The Duke family traveled to Europe in the summer of 1923 while their recently purchased Rough Point home was being renovated.

38. "Americans to Attend the First Royal Court," *New York Times*, May 9, 1930; similarly, "New York Girls at St. James' Court," *New York Times*, May 11, 1930. See also Time 15 (May 26, 1930).

39. John Sweetman, *The Oriental Obsession: Islamic Inspiration in British and American Art and Architecture, 1500–1920* (Cambridge: Cambridge University Press, 1988), 189ff.

40. As proposed by Carol Bier in Sharon Littlefield, *Doris Duke's Shangri La*, xiv. In fact, it seems unlikely that Doris Duke was in London during the exhibition, which ran from January 7 through March 7. On February 11, 1931, Doris Duke is mentioned in the society pages of the *New York Times* as being in Palm Beach. During the week of April 20, she attended the dedication of Duke University School of Medicine and Duke Hospital, as reported in Time magazine; see "Education: In a Carolina Forest," Time 17 (April 27, 1931), in which it is also noted that Nanaline Duke (whose portrait is on the cover), the only female member of the Duke University Board of Trustees, was not at the ceremony because she was in Europe. It seems more likely that Doris Duke may have joined her mother in London in the spring of 1931. According to the *New York Times*, Mrs. Duke returned to America from London on July 15, 1931, while her daughter arrived in New York on a ship from Plymouth and Le Havre on September 10, 1931, as reported on those respective dates. Even if Doris Duke arrived in London only after the exhibition had closed, it is likely she encountered some of its afterglow given its enormous popularity; copies of the London Times Persian art supplement, dated January 5, 1931, with the model of the Masjid-i Shah on the cover, as well as other exhibition-related materials, survived beyond the run of the exhibition, as many of them became collector's items. See Barry Wood, "'A Great Symphony of Pure Form': The 1931 International Exhibition of Persian Art and its Influence," Ars Orientalis 30 (2000), fig. 1.

41. On the significance and reception of the exhibition, see Wood, "'A Great Symphony of Pure Form': The 1931 International Exhibition of Persian Art and Its Influence" and B.W. Robinson, "The Burlington House Exhibition of 1931: A Milestone in Islamic Art History" in Vernoit, *Discovering Islamic Art*, 147–55. See also Jay Gluck and Nathan Siver, eds., *Surveyors of Persian Art: A Documentary Biography of Arthur Upham Pope & Phyllis Ackerman* (Ayisha, Japan: Costa Mesa, CA-SoPA, 1996), 185ff.

42. Gluck and Siver, eds., *Surveyors of Persian Art*, 8–9.

43. Wood, "'A Great Symphony of Pure Form': The 1931 International Exhibition of Persian Art and its Influence"; Robinson, "The Burlington House Exhibition of 1931: A Milestone in Islamic Art History."

44. Stuart Cary Welch, "Private Collectors and Islamic Arts of the Book" in Toby Falk, ed., *Treasures of Islam* (London: Sotheby's/Philip Wilson Publishers, 1985), 28.

45. Correspondence from and to Pope regarding the trip is preserved in the Shangri La Historical Archives, much of it dating to January and February of 1938; see Littlefield, *Doris Duke's Shangri La*, 40.

46. See A. Bruce MacLeish and Pieter N. Roos, *Rough Point: The Newport Home of Doris Duke* (Newport: Newport Restoration Foundation, 2003) and Robert P. Foley, A. Bruce MacLeish, and Pieter N. Roos, *Extraordinary Vision: Doris Duke and the Newport Restoration Foundation* (Newport: Newport Restoration Foundation, 2010). In 1968 Duke formed the Newport Restoration Foundation, and the following year she actively began to acquire related Newport furniture and decorative arts.

47. Persian lusterware and especially tiles were actively collected in the latter half of the nineteenth century, at first in Europe and then in the United States; to accommodate this gargantuan appetite, especially for tiles, buildings in

Iran were literally stripped of their tile revetment. See Tomoko Masuya, "Persian Tiles on European Walls: Collecting Ilkhanid Tiles in Nineteenth-Century Europe," Ars Orientalis 30 (2000), 39–54. Many of these same tiles found their way to America, for example the luster mihrab from Veramin acquired by Doris Duke (48.327), here illustrated on page 103. On collecting fashions and taste in Persian pottery, see Oliver Watson, Ceramics from Islamic Lands (New York: Thames & Hudson, 2004), 14ff., in which he notes that the interest in mina'i followed lusterware by a few decades, only beginning in the second decade of the twentieth century. Spanish lusterware, so-called Hispano-Moresque, has already been considered in the context of the Havemeyers' collecting; see Frelinhuysen, et al., Splendid Legacy, 103, where it is noted that the Havemeyers seem to have made their collecting choices based on a similarity of palette with the probable aim of displaying their collection as a group in their dining room. The wide-scale acquisition of Iznik ware, including tiles, also began in the second half of the nineteenth century. In America, Lockwood de Forest (1850–1932), for a time a partner with Tiffany in an interior-decorating firm, acquired Ottoman, especially Syrian, tiles on his travels to the Middle East, which he sold largely for the purpose of decorating mansions and hotels. See Roberta A. Mayer, Lockwood de Forest: Furnishing the Gilded Age with a Passion for India (Newark: University of Delaware Press, 2008), 120. Exemplifying the taste for Middle Eastern rooms, often fanciful creations, and in addition to the rooms designed for the Havemeyer home, as noted above, there was the Deanery at Bryn Mawr College, designed by Lockwood de Forest in 1894, which included inlaid Syrian furniture; see Anne Suydam Lewis, Lockwood de Forest: Painter, Importer, Decorator (Huntington, NY: Heckscher Museum, 1976), 26. On the Moorish smoking room, from the Rockefeller house and now in the Brooklyn Museum, see Sweetman, The Oriental Obsession, 229 and figs. 140 and 228.

48. See Sweetman, The Oriental Obsession, 189ff., for the British domestic examples, and 221ff., for the American examples. See also Mayer, Lockwood de Forest: Furnishing the Gilded Age, 161ff., for de Forest's American commissions, and 13ff., for the interior decoration of de Forest's New York home.

49. The personal papers of Charles Lang Freer, including correspondence, diaries, art inventories, etc., are preserved in the archives of the Smithsonian Institution; for his correspondence with Whistler, see Linda Merrill, ed., With Kindest Regards: The Correspondence of Charles Lang Freer and James McNeil Whistler, 1890–1903 (Washington, DC: Smithsonian Institution Press, 1995). For Louisine Havemeyer's privately printed memoirs, see Susan Alyson Stein, ed., Sixteen to Sixty: Memoirs of a Collector (New York: Ursus Press, 1993). In addition, the Havemeyer family papers related to art collecting are preserved in the Metropolitan Museum of Art archives.

50. There is also the correspondence related to acquisitions and commissions for Shangri La's interiors, much of it written by Duke's first husband, James Cromwell, and a few auction catalogues (with annotations in her own hand), which are kept at Shangri La. There are several articles in popular magazines, one even written by Duke: See Doris Duke, "My Honolulu House," Town & Country 101 (August 1947); 73–77; see also "Miss Doris Duke and Her House in Hawaii," Vogue 148 (November 1966), 32–37.

51. Last Will and Testament of Doris Duke, Section Two, Part F, nos. 1–3 and Second Codicil to Last Will and Testament of Doris Duke, Honolulu, January 11, 1965, Section 3.

COMMISSIONING ON THE MOVE: THE CROMWELLS' TRAVELS AND PATRONAGE OF "LIVING TRADITIONS" IN INDIA, MOROCCO, AND IRAN

I am grateful to the many individuals who facilitated my research in Morocco in the fall of 2011, including Nadia Erzini; Mahan Khejenoori; the Arabesque workshop, especially Reda Naji; and various guides and hosts in Rabat, Fez, and Marrakesh. Thanks are also due to Dawn Sueoka, consulting archivist, Shangri La, for fielding many requests for this essay.

1. For an overview of traditional Moroccan crafts, see André Paccard, Traditional Islamic Craft in Moroccan Architecture (Saint-Jorioz, France: Atelier 74, 1980), 2 vols.

2. For the Moroccan Court, see, among others, Margot Adler, "'Art of the Arab Lands' Displays a Global Heritage," NPR, November 4, 2011, accessed November 13, 2011, http://www.npr.org/2011/11/04/141987063/art-of-the-arab-lands-displays-a-global-heritage; Randy Kennedy, "History's Hands," New York Times, March 17, 2011, accessed November 13, 2011, http://www.nytimes.com/2011/03/20/arts/design/metropolitan-museums-moroccan-courtyard-takes-shape.html?pagewanted=all; and Walter Denny, "The Met Resets a Gem," Saudi Aramco World 62, no. 6 (November–December 2011): 36–43.

3. "'The idea was to create this Islamic space to show the living traditions of the Islamic world [emphasis added], and also to create an area where you don't have to look at anything,' Haidar says. 'You don't have to read a label; you can sit on the bench, relax, look at the fountain.'" Navina Haidar, quoted from Adler, "'Art of the Arab Lands' Displays a Global Heritage."

4. Thalia Kennedy, "Honeymoon Chronology (more detailed for India section)," unpublished internal document, Doris Duke Foundation for Islamic Art (DDFIA), August 2011.

5. Ibid.

6. "Richest Girl May Build 'Taj Mahal' on Property Here," Palm Beach Times, April 23, 1935. For James Cromwell's discussion of the Taj Mahal as the source of his wife's inspiration, see extract of letter from James Cromwell to Eva Stotesbury, Calcutta, April 1937, 1.

7. Extract of letter from James Cromwell to Eva Stotesbury, Calcutta, April 1937, 2.

8. For the Blomfields, particularly Charles George, see Giles Tillotson, "CG Blomfield: Last Architect of the Raj," South Asian Studies 24, no. 1 (2008): 133–39.

9. Letter from F. B. Blomfield, Prem House Connaught Place, New Delhi, to James H. R. Cromwell Esquire, c/o Thos. Cook & Son Ltd., Hong Kong, July 4, 1935, 1. The Blomfield proposal also called for two major plasterwork elements — cornices and ceilings — which were cast by a firm in New York. See Don J. Hibbard, 'Shangri-La: Doris Duke's Home in Hawaii," November 2001, unpublished internal manuscript, DDFIA, annotated by Sharon Littlefield in 2006, 155, and Sharon Littlefield, "Chronology of Doris Duke's bedroom, bathroom, and dressing room," unpublished internal document, DDFIA, September 2007.

10. C. G. and F. B. Blomfield, Estimate No. 1 — Bath Room, 1.

11. Letter from F. B. Blomfield, Prem House Connaught Place, New Delhi, to James H. R. Cromwell Esquire, c/o Thos. Cook & Son Ltd., Hong Kong, July 4 1935, 1–2.

12. "Duke Millions Save Hindu Art," New York Post, May 29, 1935; this newspaper clipping appears in the Cromwells' India scrapbook and is reproduced here on page 94.

13. For the popular legacy of the Taj Mahal during the nineteenth and twentieth centuries, see Pratapaditya Pal, et al., Romance of the Taj Mahal (London: Thames & Hudson; Los Angeles: Los Angeles County Museum of Art, 1989) and Ebba Koch, The Complete Taj Mahal and the Riverfront Gardens of Agra (London: Thames & Hudson, 2006).

14. Thalia Kennedy's forthcoming essay devoted to the marble commission will illuminate this issue, as well as provide further information on F. B. Blomfield, the Indian craftsmen, Mughal design prototypes, and comparable projects of the day. See Thalia Kennedy, "Gandhi and Doris Duke: Revitalization of a Crafts Tradition," forthcoming essay in Shangri La Working Papers in Islamic Art. The author thanks Ms. Kennedy for identifying Imre Schwaiger in the photograph on pages ii–iii in this book.

15. Letter from W. D. Cross, Jr., Attorney-in-fact for Mrs. Doris Duke Cromwell, to C. G. and F. B. Blomfield, Architects, New Delhi, March 22, 1937.

16. For the itinerary, see Thos. Cook & Son Ltd. itinerary for Tour No. 2079/W. I am grateful to Dawn Sueoka for bringing this itinerary to my attention.

17. Vivien Hamilton, Joseph Crawhall, 1861–1913: One of the Glasgow Boys (London: Murray in association with Glasgow Museums and Art Galleries, 1990), 73.

18. For a photograph of Duke and Edgar Selwyn in 1938, see Life, July 25, 1938, where the caption reads, "Selwyn's company, M-G-M, is screen-testing Mrs. Cromwell."

19. "Newlywed Heiress, Here on Honeymoon, Joins Filmdom's New Year Gayety," Los Angeles Times, January 8, 1936.

20. Letter from Nigel d'Albini Black-Hawkins to James Cromwell, November 9, 1937, 5. The identity of this villa remains unknown. It seems likely that the Cromwells were led to it by Mr. and Mrs. Black-Hawkins, who appear to be their hosts in the film footage.

21. Today, the store at 14, souk Semarine is run by Hadj el-Mahdjoub Bouzian's son. I am grateful for the welcome in the fall of 2011. For further information on the carpets, see letters from Nigel d'Albini Black-Hawkins to James Cromwell, November 9, 1937, February 18, 1938, and March 31, 1938.

22. For these other projects, see the Martin letters dated December 16, 1937 and June 21, 1938.

23. René Martin, Images de Rabat: Texte et dessins de René Martin (Casablanca: Éditions Réalisations, 1938).

24. Given this seemingly anti-Orientalist stance, it is unlikely that the René Martin in question and the René Martin who painted a series of Moroccan female nudes in the 1930s and supposedly died in 1977 are one and the same. This acknowledged, a number of parallels — such as the fact that both Martins signed their names in full capital letters — raise further questions. According to the owner of 23, souk el Ghzel the Martin of 21, souk el Ghzel died in Rabat approximately six months before Independence (November 1956) and was buried in the city's Christian cemetery.

25. For chemmassiat, see Paccard, Traditional Islamic Craft, vol. 2, 158–71.

26. Jean Gallotti, Le Jardin et la Masion Arabes au Maroc (Paris: A. Lévy, 1926). For the Gallotti references, see "Memorandum of material furnished by M. Martin," October 7, 1937.

27. Although Martin was the proprietor of his eponymous firm and the main point of contact for the Cromwells, he appears to have delegated much of the work for Shangri La

to a colleague in S.A.L.A.M. René Martin. Writing from Capri, he noted, "I have given by air mail my instructions to my designer who has charge of the Cromwell villa [emphasis added]." Given that P. Vary signed the watercolors of the living room and foyer, we can assume that he was the designer in question. Letter from René Martin to James Cromwell, August 16, 1937.

28. For examples, see Paccard, *Traditional Islamic Craft*, vol. 2, 426–51.

29. Letterhead from May 1940 features the address "4, Rue Berge, just across from the Hotel Balima." Efforts to locate this studio were unsuccessful.

30. For helping me to locate 21, souk el Ghzel, I am grateful to our exceptional guide in Rabat, Fouad Hommani. For kindly offering us a tour of the home, I thank the current tenant. I am equally indebted to Martin's neighbor for the tour of his home and for sharing his memories.

31. The tilework decorating the jam of one of the arches in 23, souk el Ghzel is dated 1313/1895.

32. Oral history provided by the owner of 23, souk el Ghzel, to whom I express my sincerest gratitude.

33. For a list of such alterations, see "Memorandum on material furnished by M. Martin," October 7, 1937.

34. Personal observations of Mohammed Eissaoui Telmsani, through translator Reda Naji, Fez, November 2011. I am grateful to Reda Naji for kindly interviewing his great-uncle on my behalf, especially during the Eid holiday. As with any oral history, however astute and detailed, this account requires external verification. For more on the Najis, see "Arabesque and Moresque: The Naji Family," *Tharawat Magazine* 11 (July–September 2011): 64–66.

35. Ibid.

36. For further information on the 1938 trip, see "1938 Journey to the Middle East," Duke University Libraries, accessed November 13, 2011, http://exhibits.library.duke.edu/exhibits/show/dorisduke/doris-duke/interactive-map.

37. For a detailed examination of the tilework commission, as well as the general history of Shangri La's "Persianization" between ca. 1937 and 1940, see Keelan Overton, "From Pahlavi Isfahan to Pacific Shangri La: Reviving, Restoring and Reinventing Safavid Aesthetics, c. 1920–1940," *West 86th: A Journal of Decorative Arts, Design History, and Material Culture* 19, no. 1 (Spring–Summer 2012): 61–87.

38. Ibid., 66–67.

39. Western Union cablegram from Arthur Upham Pope to Ayoub Rabenou, January 24, 1938.

40. Preliminary contract with Ayoub Rabenou, "Vendu a Mr. Cromwell," Isfahan, April 13, 1938, 3.

41. It is likely that the Isfahani workshop was involved in the extensive restoration efforts that transpired in Isfahan just before and concurrent to the Hawai'i commission. For further information, see Overton, "From Pahlavi Isfahan to Pacific Shangri La," 63–66. For an additional contemporary account of the workshop, as being in the "house" of "the most enterprising dealer in town," see Donald Wilber, *Adventures in the Middle East: Excursions and Incursions* (Princeton, NJ: Darwin, 1986), 77–78. For Wilber's encounter with Doris Duke Cromwell, see ibid., 68. I am grateful to Jonathan Bloom for bringing this source to my attention.

42. Letter from Thos. Cook & Son to Mr. William Cross, Jr., Honolulu, March 11, 1938.

43. Letter from James Cromwell to F. B. Blomfield, January 7, 1939.

COLLECTING FOR DESIGN: ISLAMIC ART AT DORIS DUKE'S SHANGRI LA

1. For an indication of the appearance of the original entry, see archival photographs PH.SL007xx and PH.SL007ss.

2. See PH.SL0I700, ca. 1941, which shows a detail of the metal screens, prior to their removal, with more mature plantings.

3. H. D. Baker, "Memorandum of items of work to be done as of April 12, 1939," 9. "Mrs. Cromwell contemplates purchasing a Persian tile gateway to place in present location of bamboo gate." The gateway was sold to Duke as a sixteenth-century piece, but it has since been attributed a nineteenth-century date. See also letter from Ayoub Rabenou to Mary Crane, October 26, 1939.

4. Letter from James Cromwell to William Dodsworth, September 21, 1939; letter from Ayoub Rabenou to Mary Crane, October 26, 1939; letter from James Cromwell to William Dodsworth, December 29, 1939. It is not known why Duke was determined to purchase the case. Whether or not she realized it at the time of purchase, the growth of the paired Chinese banyans and bird-of-paradise, which constituted the main plantings of the garden, would soon have seemed out of scale with the bamboo entry.

5. See Don Hibbard, "Shangri-La: Doris Duke's Home in Hawaii," November 2001, unpublished internal manuscript, DDFIA, annotated by Sharon Littlefield in 2006, 27, and also Sharon Littlefield, "Mughal Garden (Allee), Tennis Court, and Monkey Cages Chronology," unpublished internal report, DDFIA, September 2007. The gap between the purchase and installation dates may be attributed to delays in shipping and receiving the tile gateway in Honolulu as well as to the diminished activity that took place at the estate during World War II.

6. See PH.SL051j, which shows the recently completed wall.

7. The relocation of the tile gateway to the dining room lanai prompted an architectural renovation to make the existing entryway fit the shape and size of the tile gateway. The entry from the lanai to the garden beyond was originally of towering height, an effect now lost with the much smaller doorway of the tile gateway. See PH.SL003z and PH.SL026h for indications of the shape and scale of the passage from the dining room lanai to the moon garden.

8. The large tile spandrels (object numbers 48.455 and 48.456) were purchased in 1962 from C. K. Kevorkian in Paris. The tile gateway may have been relocated from the garden to the dining room lanai in consequence of the purchase of the spandrels, but the sequence cannot be categorically proven. See letter from C. K. Kevorkian to Pete Cooley of the Duke Business Office in New York, October 29, 1962. Presently, the tiles are temporarily de-installed for conservation reasons and are expected to be re-installed in the Mughal Garden upon completion of treatment.

9. See Littlefield, "Chronologies for Living Room and Mihrab Room and Foyer."

10. Object numbers 48.93, 48.12.1–4, 48.87.1–2, and 48.91.1–2.

11. Tile panels are object numbers 48.82.1–2, 48.83.1–4, and 48.84.1–2.

12. For an indication of this arrangement, see PH.SL026c.

13. Object number 48.407. See PH.SL017m, among others.

14. Object numbers 48.100a–c. See letter from Thos. Cook and Son (New York) to William L. Baldwin at the Duke

Business Office in New York, September 29, 1941. This letter states that the thirteenth-century tiles were expected to arrive in New York in early October 1941 and would be shipped to Honolulu soon after.

15. See receipt from Ayoub Rabenou, 1938. Approximately sixteen meters of tile were purchased from Mahboubian, which appears to be the total quantity of the tiles.

16. The following purchases appear to be the bulk of the remaining tiles which would be installed in the courtyard: sixty-two tiles from C. K. Kevorkian, July 31, 1957; twenty tiles from C. K. Kevorkian, November 24, 1962; thirty tiles from Daniel Brooks Inc., November 8, 1965; and Sotheby's sales of the Hagop Kevorkian Collection, December 14–15, 1962, and February 25–26, 1966.

17. Includes object numbers 48.80.1–2, 48.81, 48.85.1–2, 48.92.1–2, 48.96, 48.97.1–2.

18. Object number 48.348.

19. Oral history related by Jin de Silva.

INVENTIVE SYNTHESIS: THE ARCHITECTURE AND DESIGN OF SHANGRI LA

1. Extract from a letter from James H. R. Cromwell in India to Eva Stotesbury, undated, Shangri La Archives, Honolulu.

2. Horace Trumbauer had also designed the Fifth Avenue mansion of Duke's father, James B. Duke, in 1912.

3. For photographs of the Moorish Tea House, see the Robert Yarnell Richie digital photographic collection, DeGolyer Library, Central University Libraries, Southern Methodist University, Dallas.

4. Letter from Eva Stotesbury to Maurice Fatio, May 23, 1935, Doris Duke Archives, Duke University, Durham, North Carolina.

5. Letter from Maurice Fatio, December 13, 1921, as quoted by Eric Egan in Alexandra Fatio, ed., *Maurice Fatio: Architect* (New York: A. Fatio, 1992), 5.

6. Doug Stewart, "Doris Duke's Islamic Art Retreat," *Smithsonian*, March 2004, accessed March 12, 2012, http://smithsonianmagazine.com/arts-culture/retreat.html.

7. *Honolulu Advertiser*, September 19, 1935.

8. Margaret Leech, "Profiles: Romance, Incorporated," *New Yorker* 3 (February 4, 1928), 21–23.

9. In 1944 William Johnson, who had worked for the firm since 1925, became a partner, and the firm's name changed to Wyeth, King & Johnson.

10. Marion Sims Wyeth, as quoted in Christine Davis, "Marion Sims Wyeth," *Palm Beach Post*, January 22, 2006, 22.

11. "The Alice Foote MacDougall Coffee Shops," *Architecture* 53 (January 1926): 15–17.

12. Such retractable windows were also used in Keck and Keck's 1937 Cahn House in Lake Forest, Illinois.

13. Doris Duke, "My Honolulu House," *Town & Country* 101 (August 1947), 73–77.

CONTEMPORARY ARTISTS RESPOND TO SHANGRI LA

1. Jalal Toufic, "Forthcoming," *The Withdrawal of Tradition Past a Surpassing Disaster*, PDF produced by Forthcoming Books, 2009, 57.

213

IMAGE CREDITS

Endpapers (front and back): Tim Street-Porter 2011; i: Doris Duke Photograph Collection, Doris Duke Charitable Foundation Historical Archives, David M. Rubenstein Rare Book & Manuscript Library, Duke University; ii–iii: Doris Duke Photograph Collection (top), Doris Duke Papers on the Shangri La Residence, Doris Duke Charitable Foundation Historical Archives, David M. Rubenstein Rare Book & Manuscript Library, Duke University (bottom left and bottom right); iv–vi: Doris Duke Photograph Collection; vii: Doris Duke Papers; viii: Doris Duke Photograph Collection (top); Shangri La Historical Archives, Doris Duke Foundation for Islamic Art, Honolulu, Hawai'i (bottom); ix: Doris Duke Papers; x–xi: Doris Duke Photograph Collection, photo by Martin Munkácsi; xii: Doris Duke Photograph Collection; xiii: Hawai'i State Archives, photo by Nate Farbman; xiv–xv: Doris Duke Photograph Collection, photo by Martin Munkácsi; xvi: Shangri La Historical Archives, photo by Martin Munkácsi; page 2: Street-Porter 2011 (64.17.1); page 4: Street-Porter 2011 (48.327 and 67.49); page 6: Street-Porter 2011 (64.30a–b); pages 8–9: Street-Porter 2011; pages 10–15: Street-Porter 2011; page 16: Street-Porter 2011 (54.6.1–4); pages 17–22: Street-Porter 2011; page 23: Street-Porter 2011 (64.18); page 24: Street-Porter 2011 (64.9.1); page 25: Street-Porter 2011; page 26: Street-Porter 2011 (48.33, 47.39, 47.41, and 83.3); pages 27–29: Street-Porter 2011; page 30: Street-Porter 2011 (65.109); pages 31–33: Street-Porter 2011; page 34: Street-Porter 2011 (52.28.1a–b); pages 35–42: Street-Porter 2011; page 43: Street-Porter 2011 (48.454); pages 44–45: Street-Porter 2011; page 46: Street-Porter 2011 (85.34 and 54.148); pages 47–50: Street-Porter 2011; page 51: Street-Porter 2011 (67.3a–b); page 52: Street-Porter 2011 (41.51.2); pages 53–69: Street-Porter 2011; pages 72–74: Doris Duke Photograph Collection; page 75: Doris Duke Photograph Collection (top and bottom left); Hawai'i State Archives, photograph by Nate Farbman (bottom right); page 76: Shangri La Historical Archives, gift of Hope Cromwell Hopkins; page 77: Doris Duke Photograph Collection; page 78: Shangri La Historical Archives; page 79: © 2004 David Franzen (48.168); page 80: © 2009, Doris Duke Foundation for Islamic Art, Honolulu, Hawai'i, photo by David Franzen (64.17.1); page 81: © 2011, Doris Duke Foundation for Islamic Art, Honolulu, Hawai'i, photo by David Franzen (48.347) (top); Courtesy of Sotheby's Picture Library (bottom); page 82: © 2002 David Franzen

(64.16); page 83: © 2009, Doris Duke Foundation for Islamic Art, Honolulu, Hawai'i, photo by David Franzen (41.62.3) (top); © 2009, Doris Duke Foundation for Islamic Art, Honolulu, Hawai'i, photo by David Franzen (81.49) (bottom); page 84: © 2007 David Franzen (44.4a–b); page 85: © 2009, Doris Duke Foundation for Islamic Art, Honolulu, Hawai'i, photo by David Franzen (64.48.1); page 86: © 2010, Doris Duke Foundation for Islamic Art, Honolulu, Hawai'i, photo by David Franzen (48.327); page 87: © 2007 David Franzen (48.41a–b); page 88: Shangri La Historical Archives (top); © 1999 David Franzen (bottom); page 89: © 1999 David Franzen; pages 91–92: Shangri La Historical Archives; page 94: Shangri La Historical Archives, gift of Hope Cromwell Hopkins; page 95: Keelan Overton 2009; page 96: Street-Porter 2011; page 98: Doris Duke Photograph Collection; page 99: Street-Porter 2011; page 100: Keelan Overton 2011; page 101: René Martin 1938 (top); Keelan Overton 2011 (bottom); pages 102–103: Street-Porter 2011; pages 104–105: Keelan Overton 2011; page 106: Shangri La Historical Archives, P. Vary, S.A.L.A.M. René Martin; page 107: Doris Duke Photograph Collection; pages 108–109: Shangri La Historical Archives; page 110: Keelan Overton 2009; page 111: Street-Porter 2011 (48.93); page 112: Doris Duke Photograph Collection; pages 114–117: Shangri La Historical Archives, Wyeth & King, Architects; page 118: Shangri La Historical Archives; page 120: Doris Duke Photograph Collection (left); © 2003 David Franzen (48.454) (right); page 121: Doris Duke Photograph Collection (left); © 2006 David Franzen (right); pages 122–123: © 2008 David Franzen (48.455); page 124: Shangri La Historical Archives; page 125: Doris Duke Photograph Collection (top); © 2003 David Franzen (48.84.1) (bottom); page 126: Doris Duke Photograph Collection; page 127: © 2005 David Franzen (48.100a–c); page 128: © 2006 David Franzen; page 129: Doris Duke Photograph Collection; page 130: © 2010, Doris Duke Foundation for Islamic Art, Honolulu, Hawai'i, photo by David Franzen (48.438); page 131: Street-Porter 2011; page 133: Shangri La Historical Archives; page 134: Horst / Vogue; © Condé Nast; page 136: © 2004 David Franzen (44.42a–b) (left); © 2006 David Franzen (47.120a–b) (right); page 137: © 2003 David Franzen (34.8); pages 138–139: © 2005 David Franzen (10.12); page 140: © 2008 David Franzen (48.106) (top); © 2011, Doris Duke Foundation for Islamic Art, Honolulu, Hawai'i, photo by David Franzen (48.34) (bottom); page 141: © 2007 David Franzen (48.114); page 142: Street-Porter 2011; page 143: © 2003 David Franzen (48.43); page 144: © 2007 David Franzen (48.209); page 145: Street-Porter 2011 (48.310); pages 146–147: © 2011, Doris Duke Foundation for Islamic Art, Honolulu, Hawai'i, Photo by David Franzen (65.18); page 148: © 2002 Shuzo Uemoto (54.136.1) (top); © 2011, Doris Duke Foundation for Islamic Art, Honolulu, Hawai'i, photo by David Franzen (54.2.1) (bottom); page 149: © 2011, Doris Duke Foundation for Islamic Art, Honolulu, Hawai'i, photo by David Franzen (65.63); page 150: Photo by Richard Walker. ©2003 Doris Duke Charitable Foundation (PH.DD112) (57.74); page 151: Photo by Richard Walker. ©2003 Doris Duke Charitable Foundation (PH.DD112) (57.59); page 152: © 2004 David Franzen (86.100); page 153: © 2007 David Franzen (81.15); page 154: © 2006 David Franzen (41.9) (top); © 2010, Doris Duke Foundation for Islamic Art, Honolulu, Hawai'i, photo by David Franzen (57.5) (bottom); pages 155–156: © 2011, Doris Duke Foundation for Islamic Art, Honolulu, Hawai'i, photo by David Franzen (57.54); page 157: © 2011, Doris Duke Foundation for Islamic Art, Honolulu, Hawai'i, photo by

David Franzen (57.49a–b) (top); © 2010, Doris Duke Foundation for Islamic Art, Honolulu, Hawai'i, photo by David Franzen (44.18a–b) (bottom); page 158: Doris Duke Photograph Collection, photo by Martin Munkácsi; page 159: © 2006 David Franzen (85.81); page 160: © 2004 David Franzen (64.94a–b); page 161: © 2005 David Franzen (54.220) (left); © 2011, Doris Duke Foundation for Islamic Art, Honolulu, Hawai'i, photo by David Franzen (54.98) (right); page 162: © 2007 David Franzen (48.36) (left); © 2011, Doris Duke Foundation for Islamic Art, Honolulu, Hawai'i, photo by David Franzen (47.8) (right); page 163: Street-Porter 2011 (48.351 and 54.156); page 164: Street-Porter 2011; page 165: © 2011, Doris Duke Foundation for Islamic Art, Honolulu, Hawai'i, photo by David Franzen (48.5.1); page 166: © 2008 David Franzen (48.110) (top); © 2011, Doris Duke Foundation for Islamic Art, Honolulu, Hawai'i, photo by David Franzen (48.385) (bottom); page 167: Street-Porter 2011; page 168: © 2011, Doris Duke Foundation for Islamic Art, Honolulu, Hawai'i, photo by David Franzen (47.37.3a–b; front and back); page 169: © 2006 David Franzen (83.23); pages 170–171: © 2011, Doris Duke Foundation for Islamic Art, Honolulu, Hawai'i, photo by David Franzen (65.107); page 172: © 2010, Doris Duke Foundation for Islamic Art, Honolulu, Hawai'i, photo by David Franzen (47.23) (top); © 2010, Doris Duke Foundation for Islamic Art, Honolulu, Hawai'i, photo by David Franzen (57.43) (bottom); page 173: © 2004 David Franzen (64.34a–b); page 174: Street-Porter 2011; pages 176–177: Shangri La Historical Archives, Marion Sims Wyeth, Wyeth & King, Architects; page 178: Shangri La Historical Archives, Marion Sims Wyeth, Wyeth & King, Architects (top); Shangri La Historical Archives, Wyeth & King, Architects (bottom); page 179: Shangri La Historical Archives, P. Vary, S.A.L.A.M. René Martin; page 180: Doris Duke Photograph Collection; page 181: Shangri La Historical Archives; page 183: Marion Sims Wyeth Architectural Collection, Preservation Foundation of Palm Beach Archives, Palm Beach, Florida (top); Courtesy Historical Society of Palm Beach County (bottom); page 184: Courtesy Historical Society of Palm Beach County; page 185: Marion Sims Wyeth Architectural Collection, Preservation Foundation of Palm Beach Archives, Palm Beach, Florida; pages 186–189: Courtesy Historical Society of Palm Beach County; pages 190–191: Marion Sims Wyeth Architectural Collection, Preservation Foundation of Palm Beach Archives, Palm Beach, Florida; page 192: Courtesy Historical Society of Palm Beach County; page 193: Marion Sims Wyeth Architectural Collection, Preservation Foundation of Palm Beach Archives, Palm Beach, Florida; pages 194–195: Marion Sims Wyeth Architectural Collection, Preservation Foundation of Palm Beach Archives, Palm Beach, Florida; pages 196–197: Shangri La Historical Archives, H. Drewry Baker, Wyeth & King, Architects; page 198, Courtesy Historical Society of Palm Beach County; pages 199–200: Shangri La Historical Archives, H. Drewry Baker, Wyeth & King, Architects; page 201: © 2011, Doris Duke Foundation for Islamic Art, Honolulu, Hawai'i, photo by David Franzen; pages 202–203: Maynard L. Parker, photographer. Courtesy of the Huntington Library, San Marino, California; page 203: Street-Porter 2011; pages 204–205: Photos by Afruz Amighi; page 206: Courtesy of Emre Hüner and RODEO; page 207: Photo by David Franzen; page 208: Courtesy of Walid Raad. Original photos courtesy of David Franzen; page 209: Photos by David Adams; page 210: Street-Porter 2011; page 214: Street-Porter 2011.

LEFT Bathroom in the Mughal Suite.

ENDPAPERS Detail of the dressing room ceiling in the Mughal Suite.

DORIS DUKE'S
SHANGRI LA

EXHIBITION SCHEDULE

Museum of Arts and Design
New York, New York
September 7, 2012 – January 6, 2013

The Norton Museum of Art
West Palm Beach, Florida
March 16 – July 15, 2013

Nasher Museum of Art at Duke University
Durham, North Carolina
August 29, 2013 – January 5, 2014

University of Michigan Museum of Art
Ann Arbor, Michigan
January 25 – May 4, 2014

Nevada Museum of Art
Reno, Nevada
May 31 – September 7, 2014

Los Angeles Municipal Art Gallery
Los Angeles, California
October 23 – December 28, 2014

Honolulu Museum of Art
Honolulu, Hawai'i
March 4 – July 5, 2015

First published in the United States of America in 2012
by Skira Rizzoli Publications, Inc.
300 Park Avenue South
New York, New York 10010
www.rizzoliusa.com

2012 2013 2014 2015/ 10 9 8 7 6 5 4 3 2 1

Printed in China

ISBN 13: 978-0-8478-3895-0

Library of Congress Control Number: 2012938804

PROJECT EDITOR
Sandra Gilbert

ART DIRECTION
Abbott Miller and Kim Walker, Pentagram